FROM

WRECKAGE

TO SUNRISE

UNDERSTANDING THE IMPACT OF DOMESTIC ABUSE/VIOLENCE AND ADDRESSING THE PROBLEM

Veronica N. Nondabula

Disclaimer

CONTENTS

Dedication

To my wonderful, loving, caring family members, your love for me speaks volumes and reassures me of a brighter future. I could not be any prouder to be part of such an amazing unit.

To all the women who have shared their painful stories with me over the years and have allowed themselves to be vulnerable, I wish you all well and pray you find peace, joy and hope for a better and brighter future. You have inadvertently kindled a fire in me to produce this book.

To all the men who are suffering in silence from the traumatic and painful experiences of their past, that have been suppressed with periods of emotional eruption, causing harm to their loved ones. May this book provide you with a different perspective on the life's journey. I wish you all the best as you make the decision to follow the guidance and recommendations made in the book towards improving your relationship with yourself and your loved ones.

FROM WRECKAGE TO SUNRISE

Acknowledgements

To my late parents: Thank you for your immense love, prayers and kindness. You always believed in me and were always available whenever I needed you. I saw you exude affection and compassion towards those who came your way. You gave your all to ensure others were safe, warm and comfortable under your watch. Thank you for living such exceptional and exemplary lives and creating an atmosphere of unconditional love. Your seeds live forever in us.

To my siblings, nieces and nephews: I adore you, your uniqueness and your different approaches to life. Your support and belief in me have made me view life from a different perspective. I love you all greatly.

To my precious children: I am blessed to have you. Thank you for your patience, compassion and, above everything else, your love for me. Writing this book would have been more challenging had it have not been for your understanding and support. I love you more than words can express.

FROM WRECKAGE TO SUNRISE

CHAPTER 1
<u>What is domestic abuse?</u>

According to the National Coalition Against Domestic Violence, domestic abuse—also referred to as domestic violence—is "the wilful intimidation, physical assault, battery, sexual assault, and/or other abusive behaviour as part of a systemic pattern of power and control perpetrated by one intimate partner against another especially in a domestic setting, such as in marriage or cohabitation". Domestic violence also includes other forms of abuse/violence, such as emotional abuse, sexual abuse/violence, psychological abuse, spiritual abuse, reproductive coercion, financial abuse, and last but surely not least, physical abuse/violence.

Domestic violence is mostly perpetrated against women, and the frequency and severity of reported cases suggest that it is mostly done to control, suppress and dominate the victim. Children, both boys and girls, are also victims of this abuse. Domestic violence has become an epidemic that affects hundreds of thousands of individuals (known cases) around the world each year. Although domestic violence is not exclusive to any race, nationality, ethnicity, skin colour, religious stance, sexual orientation, economic or financial status, there are reasons why some people hurt others. Domestic violence has ravaged victims, exposed them, made them vulnerable to life and various situations, and sadly, it continues to this day. Most victims' lives change forever as a result, and it takes an exceptionally long period of time for some to recover following the abuse.

Types of domestic abuse/violence

It is not correct to think that abuse or violence is just about physically hitting or beating a partner or someone close, as it goes way beyond that. The thought that abuse is triggered by physical observations or actions and done physically is a shallow one; there is more depth to abuse than that. Many people do not even realise when they are perpetrating domestic violence because they may not be in a state of mind where they are aware that they are committing a crime against another human. Therefore, it is important for the perpetrator to understand how domestic violence works and the different ways in which it could be perpetrated.

Verbal abuse (Name-calling and other forms): This is often the most common form of domestic abuse. It is usually the first step and may lead to other forms of violence. Name-calling commonly arises because of misunderstandings, disagreements, stress, frustration, resentment, arguments or fighting, and it could ultimately culminate in physical violence. Name-calling is not just ethically bad, but it hurts the emotions of the victim and destroys their self-esteem and confidence. In fact, some people use this vile language towards their spouses so frequently that their children grow up believing these degrading and belittling things about their mother because they heard the father call her such.

Closely related to name-calling is body-shaming. I have seen more cases than I care to recall about people body-shaming their intimate partners to the point that some women attempt to commit suicide or become so mentally broken that it takes years of patience and hard work to restore their self-esteem—if they ever fully recover. A human body is like a piece of wood. It can be carved into something more beautiful and perfect, if approached the right way. However, some people do not see it this way, and they would rather hurt others with words because of their physical appearance. And sadly, some of these physical changes and problems are a result of the spouses' abusive behaviour towards the victim.

Physical abuse or assault: Several reports and findings made available by the United Nations and the World Health Organization on domestic violence suggest that the percentage of women who suffer some form of physical abuse from their intimate partner is as high as 70%. A slightly lesser percentage suffer direct physical violence that may range from slapping, punching, shoving, poking, assaulting with a weapon, throwing against a hard surface, spitting, biting, locking someone outside or inside the home, strangling or choking, sleep deprivation, physical restraint, etc. Physical abuse starts slowly and builds up in intensity over time until it becomes a normal routine and a cycle of violence.

It is shocking to understand that most communities—in particular, African and Asian communities—have built a culture of silence around domestic violence to the extent that the victims (and potential victims) view it as normal for their fathers, husbands or even brothers to "take a strap and correct their mistakes" or "slap some sense into them" or "talk some sense to them". Some fathers even threaten their children with "the promise" that their future husbands will hit them until they learn the lessons they are failing to learn in their youth. This is unacceptable, and these people endure significant hurt from a family that ought to be a pillar of trust and support. Physical abuse leaves the victims not only with physical scars but with deep emotional and psychological scars.

Emotional abuse: This form of abuse is carried out on an emotional level. It hurts more, but unlike physical abuse, it leaves no physical scars and is exceedingly difficult to prove. I have found that perpetrators of this form of abuse use it as their main weapon to strip their victim of their self-confidence and self-esteem and keep them feeling worthless. It is usually a blame game. They do this by constantly blaming their partners for all the problems in their lives and their relationships, constantly underplaying their partner's achievements and accomplishments, telling them they will never amount to anything good, constantly guilt-tripping, emotionally blackmailing, humiliating and intimidating their partner. Should they know about their partner's past hurtful or traumatic experiences, they use this against them by telling their partner that it was their fault they suffered abuse in their previous relationship—thereby intentionally and heartlessly inflicting more abuse and trauma on their partner.

Financial abuse: Not many people know that money can be a cause or tool for abuse. I have witnessed some astonishing cases where the perpetrators of abuse subjected their partners to financial abuse in different forms. They take over their partner's income and salary, bank accounts, and exert full control and unbearable pressure over how they spend their own money. Some even stop their wives from making any financial decisions or transactions in the family, and everything concerning money must be authorised by them.

The perpetrators often make their partners do domestic chores, perform sexual acts they do not enjoy or like, or do some other activities they are not pleased with before they are given money to take care of their personal needs. Some of the abusers would use and abuse women financially by living with them and never contributing a penny for their upkeep. This is even worse when there are children involved as the woman would have to work hard to pay the rent, bills, meet the children's needs and the adult's needs, including the abuser who would still be financially dependent on the woman. They would often drive the woman's car, never refill the petrol, and just dump it on the driveway/garage with an empty tank. In developed countries like the UK, US and some parts of Europe, these abusers go as far as using the children to generate an income from the government's benefits system by claiming child benefits, etc., especially if the partner has no recourse to public funding. These are men who never even buy a carton of milk, never mind a packet of nappies for their own children.

Sadly, this form of abuse extends to the activities that the parties may be involved in outside the family home. For example, I have seen instances involving community groups, church activities or projects where the abuser will manipulate their partner into "sponsoring" big and expensive projects, claiming that she will be reimbursed by that particular group. Should the reimbursement not happen and should she raise the matter with the abuser, he would become violent and shut the woman down by not only saying nasty things to her but also by painting her black to everyone involved in that particular activity or project.

Isolation and control: The perpetrator/abuser may prevent their partner from seeing and spending time with their family, friends, or other loved ones. This includes controlling behaviours such as constantly monitoring their phone calls, text messages and emails, deciding the people they can visit, continuously disparaging them in front of friends and family. Can you imagine someone putting a leash on you, preventing you from seeing someone you care about? This is the violation of human and social rights that millions of women across the globe find themselves facing on a daily basis. I have seen perpetrators spend more time on their partner's mobile phones and social media accounts than they spend on their own devices. They want to have access to every piece of information that their partner possesses to feed their selfish egos and twist and wrongly interpret what is presented before them to aid their ultimate goal, which is to isolate their partner and get away with it.

This behaviour includes controlling the food they eat at the family home, and if it is not cooked or prepared the way they, the perpetrator, want it, then they will criticise their partner by telling her she does not know how to cook. They may even go as far as throwing the food in their partner's face or flipping it on the table or onto the floor. It is sad to say that this behaviour is mainly exhibited by men who do not do any household chores, who don't even know how to fry an egg, not to mention cook a meal. They may also control their partner's style of dressing and demand that she changes her wardrobe to suit their own fantasy style of what their partner should look like. If they buy an item for their partner, they will only compliment her when she is wearing that particular item and they are blind to the other precious possessions that their partner has. Intriguingly, all the things that the partner is criticised, crushed and humiliated for by the abuser are the things that she is appreciated and complimented for by those in her social sphere.

Sexual abuse: It goes without saying that some perpetrators of violence use sex as a form of gaining power by being sexually violent towards their partners. It is sad to say that some men can only attain sexual orgasm if there is violence or verbal abuse during sexual intercourse. If their partners did not feel the pain or scream, they would not feel as powerful. I do not believe that women would choose to be treated in such a humiliating and dehumanising way by their partners given the options, but they probably conform to this due to their fear of the consequences should they not submit to this behaviour.

The perpetrators of abuse are very cunning and devious in their actions. They can play mind games with their partner, calling this form of abuse "making up" following an episode of their violent behaviour. They do not consider the feelings of the woman and often force themselves on her without consent. This is called *rape*, and it is not acceptable whether the couple is married or not. This should not be entertained and, like any form of abuse, should be reported to the relevant authorities. It is not right to inflict pain on another person and the same applies to the perpetrators who specialise in forcing themselves onto a woman who does not want to have sex with them or no longer enjoys sex with them because of their abusive behaviour.

The above are just a few examples of the daily forms of domestic abuse that a lot of perpetrators subject their partners to. They never put themselves in their partner's shoes because of their self-centred perspective and selfish desires. Their focus is on having their needs met by their partner, no matter how much pain they inflict on them. This is ferocious and should be stopped from happening.

Effects of domestic abuse

I would like us to look at how domestic violence can affect the perpetrator himself without realising it, how it affects the partner, the relationship or marriage, as well as the children involved in that union.

Domestic violence remains one of the major reasons why many homes are destroyed today. There is always a limit to how much pain and suffering an individual can endure before she eventually throws in the towel and makes the much-needed decision to put a stop to the abusive relationship. Domestic violence continues to ravage individuals and families across the world, cutting across race, social class, belief and status.

It is not just poor and uneducated men who commit this atrocity. It's just as common among rich and educated men of "good calibre" in society. Education is meant to make humans better in their thinking faculties, not to make them monsters and aggressors towards women and the law. However, those in positions of authority and power often use this to intimidate, oppress, disempower and eventually paralyse their partners, leaving them with no voice or say in the relationship. Everyone, including the perpetrators of violence, wants to feel safe, loved and protected. However, when people hurt those closest to them, they rob them of their dreams and aspirations.

I believe that men who dare to learn and understand how harmful domestic violence is will begin to find ways to curb and eventually end this menace. Domestic abuse/violence destroys homes, marriages and lives—for the victims and the perpetrators themselves. It does not just harm or destroy the victims and the family involved, but it also destroys the perpetrators in ways that they may not recognise, or in ways that they deny or refuse to acknowledge.

I will be talking in later chapters about some of the more obvious effects of this dangerous disease that is destroying many innocent lives in our society. To clearly distinguish how domestic violence and abuse negatively impacts both the victims and the perpetrators, I have written the effects in two different sub-sections below. I hope that as you read, you will be able to identify certain points that resonate with you and learn from them.

Effects on the victims

1.   Breaking of relationships, marriage and homes

As mentioned earlier, domestic violence is among the top reasons why relationships, marriages and homes break down. When the perpetrator continues to abuse their partner emotionally, mentally, physically and otherwise, it is only a matter of time before the partner finds the strength and courage to seek justice and take herself away from the abuse. There are countless stories from across the world, even in our own neighbourhoods, where people who seemed to have good relationships and lives lost everything they had when domestic violence began to creep in. Domestic abuse/violence affects the very foundation of a relationship and leaves irreparable damage on the victims.

Most people are surprised when they hear of a relationship breaking down, especially couples who are in the public eye or in leadership and present as though everything is all rosy and well. It goes unnoticed until the woman who suffers abuse decides to speak out or walk out of the relationship. Some women who suffer abuse from their partners tend to develop resilience and strength because of the circumstances they find themselves in. Whilst this may be the case for some women, this is in no way undermining the emotional and psychological impact of abuse on their wellbeing. This can even be more complicated when there are children involved, as the woman not only have to be strong for herself but also for her children, who may have already been exposed to the abuse in their family environment.

Things do get really challenging at the point of separation, especially when the abuser becomes more abusive/violent and dangerous towards the partner, threatening her or behaving with high levels of antagonism and resentment towards her.

2.   Destruction of trust and love

For two people to make the commitment to be in a relationship, they must have some basic common ground that their relationship is built upon. I believe that a man enters a relationship or even marries a woman he feels safe and secure with. Love and trust are the very foundations upon which relationships are built upon, and when the man abuses his wife or begins to act violently towards her, he slowly destroys that foundation of love and trust. Love is reciprocal, and when this does not happen in a relationship, the partner on the giving end becomes exhausted and drained of love.

Abusers fail to understand that women are emotional by nature, and when they love, they do it selflessly. Once this is betrayed—through abusive behaviour, in this case—the woman breaks down and ultimately reaches her emotional rock bottom. It takes a long time to rebuild from this position, and in most cases, that love and trust that once existed can never be repaired.

3.   Risk of physical injury, permanent damage and death

On the 15th of April 2020, *The Guardian* (UK edition) reported figures that were revealed to MPs by Vera Baird DBE QC, the victims' commissioner for England and Wales. It stated: "At least 16 suspected domestic abuse killings in the UK have been identified by campaigners since the Covid-19 lockdown restrictions were imposed, far higher than the average rate for the time of year, it has emerged. Karen Ingala Smith, the founder of Counting Dead Women, a pioneering project that records the killing of women by men in the UK, has identified at least 16 killings between 23 March and 12 April, including those of children". She further stated "We have to be cautious about how we talk about increases in men killing women. Over the last 10 years, in the UK, a woman has been killed by a man every three days, by a partner or ex-partner, every four days. So, if this was averaged out, we might expect to see seven women killed in 21 days. In reality, there are always times when the numbers are higher or lower".

The numbers above are typical examples of the crisis facing our society today. And although these figures only relate to UK homicides in a limited timeframe, it does make one wonder how many women are killed by violent men in a day around the world. There is a staggering number of abusers who never take responsibility for their actions and blame their violent behaviour on their partners. The NHS is dealing with large numbers of women who suffer physical diseases and illnesses as a result of their exposure to the stress and torture constantly inflicted on them by their abusive partners. Indeed, many die prematurely as a result of this inflicted pain that manifests itself in different diseases, like cancer.

All this killing starts in the mind when perpetrators begin telling their partners that they fantasise about killing them, and even disclosing how they would do it. If this is left unaddressed and unreported, or if the spouse remains in this relationship, they often end up being killed by their vicious partner who only thinks about himself and never considers the impact of his behaviour on others. Anger is an emotion that everyone has, and I am of the view that it is wrong for abusers to blame this emotion for their actions. They choose to behave in an abusive manner and to address the issues they face with anger and violence. They may blame their spouses for everything, but this does not change the fact that they are at fault by virtue of their choice to be abusive and violent instead of addressing their problems and challenges in an amicable way.

4.   Psychological damage

Safe Lives is a charity that deals directly with domestic abuse. Their view is that "Psychological abuse involves the regular and deliberate use of a range of words and non-physical actions used with the purpose to manipulate, hurt, weaken or frighten a person mentally and emotionally; and/or distort, confuse or influence a person's thoughts and actions within their everyday lives, changing their sense of self and harming their wellbeing". The perpetrators use a wide range of hidden strategies to maintain control and brainwash their partner, presenting insults as a joke, manipulating them, causing them to doubt their sanity and presenting different versions of events. I have seen this in cases where perpetrators are confronted about their behaviour, especially when they have uttered demeaning and belittling words to their partners. They quickly deny this and immediately turn the tables against their partner. They often say things like, "you are crazy", "you are screwed up", "you're a liar", etc.

The perpetrators are good at telling their partners that they are mentally unstable and there is something wrong with them. They take advantage of their partner's vulnerabilities, and those with mental health illnesses are threatened with being sectioned. Those with an insecure immigration status are threatened with deportation should they stand up for themselves and therefore are kept in bondage and continuous abuse and exploitation by the perpetrator. Things get worse if the partner gets pregnant as they are often told that should they leave the perpetrator; social services will take their child/ren away because they are not fit to care for the child/ren. These are a few examples of psychological abuse, but, of course, this could be perpetrated in many different forms, depending on the parties involved, their class and status in society.

Effects on the perpetrators

1. Guilt

I have discovered that perpetrators of domestic violence—at least, those who have a conscience—often seek refuge in particular activities to "cool off" or soothe their conscience and ease the guilt they feel. I have also come across women who stay in very abusive relationships and when asked why, they say the abusers always break down and cry to show how sorry they feel. And yet, just hours or days later, history repeats itself and the abuser's promise to never behave in that manner again is broken. This cycle goes on and on until someone, usually the partner, takes action to protect herself from suffering further harm from her abuser. Unfortunately, some abusers lose their sense of guilt due to the prolonged period of their abusive behaviour towards their partner, as well as their ex-partners. They feel that their partner deserves to be hurt, and they lose touch with the reality that they have, over some time, become a beast towards their intimate partner, who is trapped in the relationship.

2.   Trouble with the law

It is shocking to learn that at this day and age, there are places in the world where domestic violence is not a crime whilst most countries protect their citizens from domestic violence or abuse. This goes to show just how important this subject is. For example, in the US and the UK, abuse/violence towards a partner is punishable by the law. Domestic violence protection orders (DVPOs) are available across England and Wales. They can be put in place by police and magistrates as safeguards in the immediate aftermath of a domestic abuse incident. Police work hand in hand with domestic abuse services, including the courts, who can issue restraining orders to prohibit the perpetrator from returning to the place of residence and from having contact with the partner. Depending on the evidence provided by the partner, the perpetrator could face imprisonment and charges for their abusive behaviour.

3.   Destruction of social image/standing

"You also risk destroying your public image if you choose to become a perpetrator of domestic violence. Nobody wants to be associated with even a reformed serial abuser, not to mention an unashamed one".

Having seen some of the ways that domestic violence can affect lives, I am of the view that it is important for abusers to know they can overcome the cycle of abuse and live a normal life. I discovered that the perpetrators of domestic violence who still have the aptitude to reflect on their behaviour and lifestyle and acknowledge the problem do better once they choose to seek support to address this problem. It is important to be introspective and understand why perpetrators behave in the ways they do. In the next chapter, I will be guiding perpetrators of domestic violence to look inside themselves and reflect on some of the factors that could be contributing to their vicious behaviour.

CHAPTER 2
Identifying the root cause of domestic violence

In this chapter, I will be taking you on a journey of reflection and self-examination. This is quite necessary because, as mentioned earlier, perpetrators of abuse/violence have to find a way to end this vicious cycle of behaviour that is having a devastating impact on our society. In order to address any problem, one must first understand the root cause of it and acknowledge its existence. My wish is for perpetrators of abuse to be able to embark on self-reflection every now and again so they can realign their lives and make the necessary changes. I believe that, apart from having to go through the legal route—where the actions of abusers are subject to discipline in an effort to curtail this behaviour—the abusers themselves can also choose to seek support and address the problem.

Changing any behaviour or habit is not easy, so it may take a while before the desired goal is achieved. However, if one has developed a bad habit over the years that is detrimental and has a negative impact on someone else, then this should not be a mountain too tall to climb. This takes a decision that will continuously and intentionally be employed every day towards a positive outcome. I find the stories of those who make such decisions and choices to seek support to modify their behaviour and negative approach to life issues, very intriguing and inspirational.

General background on the root causes of domestic violence

As mentioned in the previous chapter, domestic violence, also known as domestic abuse, may start when the male partner feels the need to control and dominate the female. Abusers may feel this need to control their partner for various reasons, i.e., their own low self-esteem, extreme jealousy, difficulty in regulating their anger and other strong emotions, feeling inferior to their partner academically and socioeconomically. Some perpetrators have strong traditional and cultural beliefs that lead them to think that they have the right to control their partner, some have an undiagnosed personality disorder or psychological disorder, and others may have learned this behaviour from exposure to violence in their childhood and have thereby normalised it. Male children who are brought up in an environment where women are not valued or respected are more likely to adopt the same behaviour and become abusive to women when they grow up. Female children who witness domestic violence in their families are likely to be victimised by their own husbands, as they also normalise this behaviour.

For most abusers, domestic violence is not some late-life habit that they acquire when they are old or have lived many years in peace with their partner. In fact, the number of men who become abusive later in life is really low compared to those who start to be abusive as early as their teenage years. Alcohol and drug misuse may also contribute to their violent behaviour, as a drunk or high person is less likely to control their violent impulses towards their partner. However, there is no cause of domestic violence that justifies the actions of the abuser, and this should not be used as an excuse or a rationale for their behaviour. Eventually, the abuser needs to get help for their unhealthy and destructive behaviour that hurts others in their life.

A few reasons why men may become abusive/violent

1. Upbringing

How parents or primary caregivers bring up their children is particularly important, as this shapes the behaviour of the children as they develop. Whatever the children are exposed to when they are young is viewed as normal and they mostly learn through observation from their immediate family members. This starts from their family environment and extends to the outside world. For instance, if a child grows up in a family where suppression, violence, and abuse are the order of the day, they might not see anything wrong with this. Therefore, it is normalised until they find themselves in a society where such actions are not acceptable and are immoral.

Most perpetrators of abuse and violence grew up witnessing this behaviour, particularly those who grew up in places like Africa, the Caribbean and Asia, to mention a few countries. This is the reason why they have difficulty adjusting to the moral standards of the countries they find themselves in. It is even more appalling for those who do not even recognise their unhealthy childhood experiences as a problem that has influenced their own behaviours as adults. These are the most resistant and difficult ones to deal with because despite every effort made to assist them with tracing and understanding where their abusive behaviour may be coming from, is turned around and blamed on the systems of the first world countries where they now reside, i.e. Europe, Australia or the US.

Some have deep anguish about how their father violently dealt with their mother, while others acknowledge the inappropriateness of their father's behaviours but also blame their mother for being provocative to their father. This is the type of abusers who will use jargon to justify their abusive behaviour towards their partner, blaming them for being "provocative". Regrettably, these abusers have, themselves, been dealt with violently or abusively by their own father or by family members. As such, they carry the baggage of abhorrence and misplace it on innocent individuals who were not involved in their upbringing.

Until they seek support and acknowledge their problem, abusers will never deal with their behaviours and will therefore keep on hurting innocent women, as this is the only way they know to deal with challenges in their lives. This is, after all, the way they saw the important male figures in their childhood behave—manhandling and being abusive to their mother. Whilst this behaviour may have been learnt from an abusive childhood experience, I want to emphasise that there are millions of men who were subjected to the same behaviour as children but who have chosen not to replicate this, knowing its impact on the receiving end.

2.   Encouragement from female family members

In some parts of the world, women—usually the sisters and sometimes the mother of the abuser—encourage them to be physically abusive to their partner to gain respect. I have heard countless cases of women who advise their sons to occasionally spank or slap their partner in order to make them responsive to their authority. Some horrible sisters do the same, and sadly, these are the people who cause problems for their brothers, who often jump from one partner to the other. This is common when the abuser is controlled by female family members who interfere with their decision-making on a daily basis.

Due to technology, in these modern times, this behaviour knows no boundaries or distance. I have even heard stories of sisters who control what goes on in their brothers' bedrooms. That means, it is the abuser who gives their family members permission to inappropriately interfere in their personal life, causing them to be controlled and badly influenced. Some men never grow up. They remain boys in men's bodies, and that is why their behaviours never change until they decide to make the positive changes required to lead a happy and fulfilled life.

3.   The silence of family members who should speak up or intervene

Closely related to the encouragement of this nasty behaviour is the culture of silence that has been built around domestic violence. Both the victim and the perpetrator may, over time, build a culture of silence and refuse to talk about the abuse that is ongoing in their home. Some victims learn this from their childhood, and when they grow, they think it is normal for women to be subjected to abuse by men and therefore become trapped in a culture of silence that is extremely harmful.

Silence is a shocking form of encouragement. When family members blame the victim of domestic violence and abuse and tell them to tolerate the pain without speaking out, then they indirectly condone the inappropriate behaviour of the perpetrator. Silence and fear of standing up to an abusive partner inadvertently encourages them to carry on with their abuse. Some in-laws are experts at pretending that they do not hear or witness the abuse as long as it is done by their son or brother. This is common when there are cultural differences, especially if the in-laws never approved of the relationship or marriage, do not know their son's partner and family very well, or perhaps wanted him to marry someone else from their local community.

4. Religious beliefs

Whilst the Bible is against abuse and violence—and I believe that there is no religion whatsoever in the world that encourages domestic violence—abuse is prevalent among those who lead at churches and other religious gatherings today. I acknowledge that there are genuinely great leaders in churches who love their spouses and the people that God has placed under their leadership. They nurture and kind-heartedly look after them as they aught. However, there are a number of cases of abuse emerging around them nowadays. Numerous religious leaders around the world are known to give their own perverse opinions about domestic abuse, wrongly interpreting scriptures to oppress the victims. I have observed that they do this according to their backgrounds and according to the cultures and traditions of their countries of origin. Many women suffer silently in these religious settings due to the fear that is instilled in them through references to two main scriptures: "God hates divorce" and "women should submit to their husbands".

As much as this is scriptural and true, it appears that some leaders fail to view domestic abuse/violence as a problem or fully understand the root cause of it, but they are rather quick to judge and condemn the women who challenge the abusive behaviour of their spouses. Well, some of these so-called "leaders" are perpetrators of this evil themselves and they are very good at using the scripture to manipulate, torment and curse their spouses, quoting the curses of the old testament and speaking death upon their spouses day in and day out. This makes me wonder if they really understand who God, the creator, truly is.

It seems they are instead driven by their own self-centeredness and misuse what is holy to feed their evil actions. These are perpetrators who disregard abuse, even amongst the people they lead, and they often sweep this abusive behaviour under the rug and seem to be oblivious to the problem, despite seeing and knowing the impact of it on the victims.

5.   Anger management issues

The American Psychological Association defines anger as "an emotion characterised by antagonism toward someone or something you feel has deliberately done you wrong. Anger can be a good thing. It can give you a way to express negative feelings, for example, or motivate you to find solutions to problems. But excessive anger can cause problems. Increased blood pressure and other physical changes associated with anger make it difficult to think straight and harm your physical and mental health". Anger is an emotion that everybody has, and it is expressed and managed in different ways. It is related to the "fight, flight or freeze" response of the sympathetic nervous system as it prepares humans to face difficult situations.

This is where perpetrators get it wrong. They express this emotion aggressively and violently, often to the point of causing harm or committing homicide. This is due to their lack of control and making no conscious effort to manage their anger. And some still find a way to justify their behaviour by blaming their victim. As mentioned above, everyone has these emotions, but "fighting" doesn't necessarily mean being aggressive or violent towards someone else. Anger can be expressed in a positive way that combats injustice by altering some societal, community and family rules or by implementing new behavioural norms. The same applies to relationships, but it becomes problematic when it is negatively and frequently expressed by one partner to the other partner.

There have been numerous cases around the world where the male perpetrator of violence murders their wife/partner as a result of their inability to control their anger. It is sad to see the growing number children whose mothers were killed prematurely by men who, at times, decline the support that is available to help them address their problem. Because of their denial, egocentricity and pride, they refuse to acknowledge their problem and instead blame their actions on their partner. There is an abundance of support available to help with anger management, and the men who humble themselves enough to seek support benefit greatly from these services.

6.   Mental health disorders

The Harvard Mental Health Journal, in a publication on the 1ˢᵗ of January 2011, stated "Several studies that have compared large numbers of people with psychiatric disorders with peers in the general population have added to the literature by carefully controlling for multiple factors that contribute to violence. In two of the best-designed studies, investigators from the University of Oxford analysed data from a Swedish registry of hospital admissions and criminal convictions. (In Sweden, every individual has a unique personal identification number that allowed the investigators to determine how many people with mental illness were convicted of crimes and then compare them with a matched group of controls.)

In separate studies, the investigators found that people with bipolar disorder or schizophrenia were more likely—to a modest but statistically significant degree—to commit assaults or other violent crimes when compared with people in the general population. Differences in the rates of violence narrowed, however, when the researchers compared patients with bipolar disorder or schizophrenia with their unaffected siblings. This suggested that shared genetic vulnerability or common elements of social environment, such as poverty and early exposure to violence, were at least partially responsible for violent behaviour. However, rates of violence increased dramatically in those with a dual diagnosis".

Taken together with the MacArthur study, these papers have painted a more complex picture of mental illness and violence. They suggest that "violence by people with mental illness like aggression in the general population stems from multiple overlapping factors interacting in complex ways. These include family history, personal stressors (such as divorce or bereavement), and socioeconomic factors (such as poverty and homelessness). Substance abuse is often tightly woven into this fabric, making it hard to tease apart the influence of other less obvious factors".

An article titled "Identifying Violent Behaviour Using the Oxford Mental Illness and Violence Tool in a Psychiatric Ward of a German Prison Hospital", published on the 23rd of April 2019, indicated that "Violent behaviour in individuals with severe mental disorders has been widely reported. Several studies and reviews from the United States and Europe can verify this, and especially, two groups of patients (schizophrenia and bipolar disorder) are at higher risk of committing a violent crime compared to the general population. This opinion is not agreed upon by all experts in the field, due to the vast majority of individuals diagnosed with schizophrenia never committing any act of violence.

Analysing data of more than 24,000 cases of schizophrenia and related disorders, Fazel et al. pointed out that the adjusted odds ratio of adverse outcomes, including violent behaviour, was 7.5 in men and 11.1 in women compared to the general population. They concluded that schizophrenia and related disorders are associated with increased rates of violent crime. In patients with bipolar disorders, the odds ratio for violent crime was 5. Recent surveys have determined a variety of risk factors for aggressive behaviour and violent crime in patients with schizophrenia and bipolar disorders, such as substance use disorder (SUD), young age, previous violent crime, male gender, and disadvantaged neighbourhoods.

Results of population-based studies suggest that there is an increased risk of violent offending and violent ideation in individuals with severe mental disorders and indicate a higher risk of homicide and violent crime, especially in individuals with schizophrenia. On the other hand, there are protective factors regarding violent behaviour, including intelligence, self-control, intimate relationship, and social network".

The research studies above are indicative of the fact that some people may commit acts of violence as a result of a mental illness, which can also be linked to their historical experiences and past actions/behaviours.

Despite all the many different forms of abuse, no one likes it when they are called or labelled as a "woman beater" or "batterer". This reflects a clear message that hurting a woman or anyone else because they do not see eye to eye with you on a particular subject is barbaric and unacceptable. It is important to know that domestic violence can be pre-meditated or impulsive. Knowing this makes it easier to learn the necessary skills perpetrators require in order to control their temperament.

CHAPTER 3
Understanding the evolution and progression of domestic violence

There is a popular saying that "you may never fully understand how something feels until you experience it". There is some element of truth in this when it comes to domestic violence. But again, there are two sides to each story: that of the victim and that of the perpetrator. Perpetrators never feel how terrible it is to live as a victim of domestic violence as they are the ones inflicting the pain and damage on the victim. They are not on the receiving end, even though they feel justified in their actions. It is for this reason that I want this chapter to be a place of reflection for perpetrators who read this book.

Domestic violence is mostly accompanied by deep emotional harm because this behaviour is used as a tool to keep the victim suppressed and trapped in a cycle of assault, battery, pain and silence. But the most appalling and horrible part of domestic abuse is that the perpetrator is often someone who is close, trusted and loved by the victim. Sometimes perpetrators get punished by the law if they are reported to the right authorities, but if not reported, then they get away with this atrocious behaviour and go on to abuse one woman after another. Either way, the impact and trauma that such abuse leaves on the hearts, minds and bodies of the victims and their loved ones take a long time to heal.

As mentioned earlier, domestic violence could be premeditated or spontaneous. But in most cases, once the first instance of domestic abuse occurs, perpetrators go on to commit it again. These incidences may be infrequent or have large stretches of time between them, but they usually continue. Ever wondered why this is? It is because it continues on like a stone being rolled downhill. It is slow at first, obstructed by obstacles, but it gets faster as it gathers momentum, and as many cases go unchecked, the momentum increases. This is what happens when perpetrators are not reported. They simply carry on with their abusive behaviour, moving from one woman to the other. Unfortunately, this often continues until such time that the perpetrator decides to not only acknowledge their problem but also take full responsibility for their behaviour. They can choose to stop this cycle by striving to make changes, by reaching out for support, and by committing to engaging with the services available to help them address their problem.

For a man to live peacefully and be a role model for his immediate family members or children, he first has to keep himself in check at all times. Self-identifying the things that can easily irritate him or the triggers that lead to his rage, which is often expressed in aggression, is key. For some perpetrators, the triggers could be alcohol intake or drug misuse, but for many, the triggers can be as simple as disagreements on a subject. There are perpetrators who are so narrowminded that their partners are not allowed to express opinions contrary to theirs. They only want to employ their oppressive ideas and opinions without considering their partner's views on the subject.

These are dominant figures who always see themselves as superior and want to control their relationship, marriage or home. Once they are challenged or prevented from ruling the roost, they become abusive towards their partner, and this often comes in an emotional and mental form, where they undermine the intelligence of their partner because they (the perpetrator) claim that they "know it all". Therefore, according to them, whatever their partner says is meaningless and they discount their partner's opinions at all costs.

This form of abuse progresses from the home setting into the community activities the couple may be involved in, as mentioned in the previous chapter. This is usually more pronounced in group settings where the couple may be taking a leadership role. I have, over the years, had the opportunity to observe this in a group setting, where the abuser's partner would express some really good ideas and suggestions on how to execute some task in order to make improvements in these settings for the benefit of the participants. Just because the suggestions are made by their partner, the abuser would completely discount them. However, if one of the group members came up with exactly the same suggestions, these would be taken on board, embraced and executed by the abuser with excessive admiration towards the member who offered up the same ideas. This is done with malice and with the aim of being spiteful towards their partner and to try and render her ideas useless so they will be criticised and disparaged when they withdraw from the group activities.

Perpetrators/abusers use this approach to destroy their partner's self-worth and reputation. They even go as far as manipulating the group members, encouraging them to not listen to the partner or not to take any instructions from her. This is part of the devious behaviour abusers use to gain power and recognition whilst hiding their abusive acts from the members of the group or organisation. They use absurdity and defamation against their partner in order to gain the recognition, esteem and reverence that they crave from the group or from the community.

It is also important to remember that domestic violence is founded on the desire to dominate, overpower, rule and control the victim, whilst the perpetrator feeds their ego. This desire to show dominance over a partner is a product of a weak and immature mind. Some perpetrators are just "boys in men's bodies". They often do not even understand the concept of manhood, not to mention the responsibilities that come with it and the dynamics of loving relationships. This leads me to believe that perpetrators of domestic violence have low self-esteem and try to raise their ego through abuse and control. Unfortunately, they remain empty and unfulfilled and always look for loopholes through which they can prey on their victims.

Of course, this does not mean that there are no sound men who are mentally mature and developed but still perpetrate domestic violence on their partners as a result of pure malevolence and obliviousness to the impact of their behaviour on their partners. I understand that in some parts of the world, there are repulsive perpetrators who, even if they go for support/counselling as a result of their abusive behaviour and perhaps the precipitating factors that may have contributed to it, still plan to continue with their abuse. These are perpetrators who reject help when they are actually in need of it. Seeking support should be intentional and should come from one's heart. With care, time and real effort, anyone can change the narrative of their life and the lives of those around them.

Some people say that if Hitler was able to reflect on the needless pain that he caused to millions of families around the world, he would have had a change of heart before things got out of hand. Perpetrators of violence behave like Hitler, and the same thought applies to them. If they would take some time to reflect on their actions—to pause and look around themselves to see how their rage is destroying their family and loved ones—they would sincerely have a change of heart and strive to make positive changes to their behaviour.

In the previous chapter, I mentioned anger as one of the contributing factors in perpetrators' abusive and violent behaviour towards their partners. In the next few paragraphs, I will delve into this subject based on my experience and observation of perpetrators over the years. Remember, when it comes to anger, it is best to start looking from the inside out, instead of blaming others for your anger outbursts. I am very mindful of the fact that perpetrators often use this as a tool to infuriate their partner, so they can turn the story around and blame their partner's reactions for their perverseness and label them as an "angry woman".

The truth is that perpetrators are always cunning and devious in their behaviours. Their aim is to ensure that they always conceal their acts and do everything possible to prompt a negative response from their partner. They may even go as far as recording these negative response/reactions as so-called "evidence". I find it intriguing to learn that the very men who have extreme anger problems, who are abusive and violent toward their partners, are very quick to capture their partner's reactions so they can have a corrupt foundation for their counter-allegations. This is common when the partner confronts the abusive behaviour and reports it to trusted people in their social network or to the relevant authorities dealing with violence. What perpetrators fail to understand is their mannerisms and body language, and that there are trained professionals who understand the mindset of abusers. Therefore, no matter how they cover up their acts and twist the evidence of the abuse they inflict, the truth always prevails.

Anger is an emotion just like any other, and with the right approach, anyone can learn to manage it without causing grief or harm to others. Of course, even the best of us can get angry, but what differentiates anger from domestic abuse and violence is how it is controlled and managed. Just to mention how important anger management is, some big companies in different parts of the world make it compulsory for their senior staff and brand representatives to take courses on anger management. Any man who cannot manage his anger cannot manage his household, not to mention employees in the business sector.

It is high time that perpetrators ask themselves what makes them so angry towards their partner that they cannot control this emotion, especially when some of them can control it in the outside world. They need to explore their frustration, personal issues, financial status and anything else that may be a contributing factor to their fury. Perpetrators also need to take time to examine themselves to figure out the little things that irritate them, i.e., the things that give vent to their nerves, the things that tip them off balance and fuel the anger that is already brewing on the inside. I have heard that some perpetrators could be annoyed by the cry of their own infants at midnight, if their partner cooks in a different way than what the perpetrator is used to, or if they cook in a manner that does not suit the perpetrator, irrespective of the family's needs. This is indeed selfishness and self–centeredness used by the perpetrator to control everything and everyone around them.

You might be wondering why I am using these insignificant points as examples, but I know from hearing countless stories of why violence comes into play that many men get irritated or frustrated over minor things, instead of calmly talking it over with their partner. They allow anger to build up until it all comes out in an explosive way that hurts the party on the receiving end. It is natural to have personal styles or differing preferences and policies in life, but in the case of perpetrators, they often demand or want things to be done their way, and if their partner does not conform to this, they kick off and behave like a beast, instead of viewing the situation from the other perspective and dealing with the matter in a non–abusive way.

Perpetrators need to think of how their unpleasant behaviour affects their partner and the children in the relationship. It seems that perpetrators who do not have children with their partner, but where she has children from a previous relationship(s), are the most selfish ones. They often exhibit more aggressive behaviour as they do not care about the impact of this on their partner's children. Instead of striving to be a role model for the children, whose fathers are already absent for different reasons, they inflict more emotional and psychological damage to those children. They are heartless and wicked in their actions.

There are countless young women who are terrified of marriage today because of their childhood experience of witnessing domestic abuse or violence in their homes. They have often seen their mother suffer from the devastating effects of abuse inflicted by their father/stepfather. Perpetrators who have male children, in particular, are unknowingly instilling the same abusive behaviour in their children, which starts to manifest itself in their late teen years into their adulthood. Whilst they have a choice to not follow their father's footsteps, most of them struggle to manage life's circumstances without resorting to violence as this is all they know.

The ultimate goal is to make the world better, not worse than it is. And in just the same way that perpetrators choose to be abusive and violent, they can also make the same choice to change the story of their lives and make things right again. Everyone can become a better man, a better lover, and a better father to the people who hold them dear. They have to seize that chance with both hands and carefully but tenaciously work towards making their family happy again. Being a loving father and a loving spouse does not reflect weakness, it shows an admirable strength. As I have highlighted in some of the root causes of abusive behaviour in chapter 2, I am of the view that, amongst other things, perpetrators of violence can follow some simple steps to begin their path to recovery.

These are guidelines that some have taken on board and have benefited from. I am also mindful of the fact that domestic violence is a worldwide issue and may be addressed differently in different parts of the world. What works in one country may not work in another. Nevertheless, if one strategy does not work, then it is wise to apply what is helpful and beneficial in one's local community. There is a vast number of resources available to help address this behaviour and its devastating impact in each and every country. All perpetrators have to do is to reach out and they will be heard.

The effects of domestic abuse on children.

The effects of domestic abuse/violence differ for each child, depending on a number of factors, such as their age, gender, race, stage of development, family environment/structure, cultural influences and resilience to trauma. Children can experience both short- and long-term cognitive, behavioural and emotional effects as a result of witnessing domestic abuse. Each child responds differently to trauma. Some may be resilient and not exhibit any negative effects. This does not mean they are not affected by the traumatic experiences they witness in their homes. It is therefore crucial to understand the emotional impact of domestic violence on children.

An article in *Educational & Child Psychology* Vol. 31 No. 1 97, published in 2014, stated "Young children who live with domestic violence represent a significantly disempowered group. Developmentally, young children have relatively limited verbal skills and emotional literacy. In addition, the context created by domestic violence frequently involves an atmosphere of secrecy and intimidation, as well as reduced emotional availability from children's main caregivers. Taken together, these factors severely restrict these young children's capacity and opportunities to make their voices and needs heard".

The article detailed a qualitative study undertaken with children who had lived with domestic violence and who were given the opportunity to share their emotional worlds through projective play and drawing assessments. "Eight children aged between 5 and 9-years-old, took part together with their mothers. Transcripts of semi-structured interviews with the mothers and projective play assessments with the children were analysed using abbreviated, social constructionist grounded theory.

Interpretations from the children's drawings served to elaborate and validate themes found in the transcript data. Themes were then linked and mapped into an initial theoretical model of how domestic violence impacts emotionally on young children. The data gathered showed that domestic violence generates a range of negative and overwhelming emotions for young children".

The model suggested that while domestic violence is ongoing, children experience repeated emotional distress and family dynamics continue to be disrupted, meaning that children were left with inadequate coping strategies and ultimately became overwhelmed. For some children, their internal chaos was represented vividly in the style of their storytelling and drawing. Others had managed to distance themselves from their overwhelming feelings, but their underlying anxieties were evident in their drawings and play. All of the mothers reported changes in their children's behaviour since they had separated from their violent partners, with children becoming more expressive in their emotions. The increased feelings of stability and security within the family overall were cited by several mothers as creating a window of possibility for change. However, many of the mothers acknowledged still feeling overwhelmed at times. It is to be expected, therefore, that children's own journeys towards emotional security were still far from being complete.

It appears that this finding disproves the suggestions that children do not notice or remember domestic violence taking place in their homes. Living with domestic violence, whether they see or hear the abuse, is overwhelming emotionally for children. Younger children exposed to domestic violence can exhibit physical problems, such as bedwetting and failure to thrive, as this is the channel through which emotional turmoil shows itself in children who lack the words to voice it. Similarly, a child's behavioural presentation can provide a useful indicator of their underlying emotional distress, although emotions, such as anxiety or unhappiness, may be displayed through different behaviours depending on the age, gender and personality of the child. Perpetrators should be fully aware of this as their behaviour not only impacts their partner, but also the children involved in that relationship.

Tamara Hill detailed nine signs of traumatic bonding in her article "Bonded to the abuser", published in Psych Central (2015). She stated, "Individuals who have bonded to their abuser often exhibit certain emotional and behavioural signs that are important for us to recognize".

I will summarise some of these behavioural and emotional signs below:

1.   Overidentifying with the abuser: Some individuals who have endured long-term abuse often find themselves harbouring conflicting emotions. There are times when the abused individual may hate the abuser one minute and then make statements or do things that makes the relationship appear better than it actually is the next minute. This seems to be more applicable to older children in their teen years and upwards.

2.   Feeling indebted to the abuser: Some abused individuals may develop a sense of gratitude for something that the abusive individual has done for them. For example, if an adolescent was once homeless and placed in multiple foster care homes but the abusive individual took them in and treated them well before the abuse, the abused individual may feel he or she owes the abuser something. Tamara mentioned that she had been

told by severely abused adolescents that the abuser "loved me or he would not have helped me".

3. Feeling that he or she "needs me": Some abused individuals develop an emotional bond with their abuser that makes them feel they sometimes owe the abuser something. For example, individuals who have been sexually, emotionally, or physically abused may find themselves feeling sorry for the emotional or psychological challenges of their abuser and develop a sense of empathy or compassion for them. This can lead to the abused individual feeling indebted to the person and dedicated to "helping them get better". This kind of behaviour can typically be found in romantic relationships in which the abused individual becomes so emotionally protective of the abuser that they will endure the abuse in order to please the abuser.

4. Explaining almost everything away: A very typical behaviour of some abused individuals is to make excuses for the abuse. The abuser doesn't hurt them because they are bad but because "I deserved it. I wasn't nice that day" or because "he was jealous, I would be too". This is often a tell-tale sign that the abused individual is bonding or bonded to their abuser.

5. Protecting the abuser: Most of us would run away from someone who is abusing us. We do not want to experience pain and we do not want to feel the shame of being abused. But sometimes, because the abuser is often mentally or emotionally disturbed and is the product of a dysfunctional environment, the abused individual can develop such a bond that they feel the need to protect the abuser. Sometimes the abused individual might stand up for the abuser and go against people who truly care. A teenage girl who has been dating an abusive boyfriend

will most likely go against her mother when her mother attempts to highlight the negative traits and behaviours in the boyfriend.

6.   Allowing the abuse to continue to "please" the abuser: Some individuals, primarily those who are being sexually abused and manipulated, will permit the abuse to continue to "keep problems down" or "please him/her". The victim becomes so overwhelmed by a failure to protect or stand up for themselves that they give in. Or the individual is fearful of walking away and remains in the situation for however long they can.

7.   Wearing multiple "hats": Depending on how emotionally or psychologically unstable the abuser is, some abused individuals will play multiple roles in the life of the abuser. For example, a child who has been physically and verbally abused by a substance–abusing parent with five other young children might begin to play the role of caregiver to the younger children, become a teacher to the kids who struggle with homework, and surrogate parent, babysitter, or therapist to the abuser, etc. Playing multiple roles often results in a lack of identity and feeling overwhelmed. Many children lose their childhood prematurely and end up developing into depressed, anxious and suicidal adults.

8.   Hiding negative emotions in the presence of the abuser: If you are sad and the abuser is happy, you hide your sadness. If you are happy and the abuser is depressed, you hide your elation. If you are feeling hopeless and depressed but your abuser is walking around the house singing and playing music, you will most likely hide your emotions and go along to get along.

9.   Desiring love and affection despite being hurt: Most individuals who are the victims of abuse desire love and

affection, sometimes only the love and affection of the abuser. It is almost as if the person desires the love and affection of the abuser so much that they will do anything to achieve it.

Trauma is often defined as a terrible event that outweighs a child's ability to cope (National Child Traumatic Stress Network, 2015). "This inability to cope often leads to mental health challenges such as anxiety, depression, and even personality disorders such as borderline personality disorder, narcissism, or avoidant personality. Even more, trauma can interfere with our ability to develop and maintain healthy relationships (work, marriage, friend, family) and appropriate social interactions. Trauma can also affect development throughout the lifespan and lead to a lifetime of emotional lability ('switchable' emotional states or moods)". This article, as summarised above, gives a clear picture of what traumatic bonding with an abuser is. Abusers often capitalise on this to make the life of their victim even more miserable given their vulnerability to abuse.

Rehabilitation Programmes

I would like to draw attention to the journal issues in 2017 that covers the piece of research and intervention undertaken with perpetrators in the UK. The International Journal of Law, Policy and the Family, Volume 31, Issue 3, December 2017 stated "Domestic violence is a destructive social harm which damages the lives and well-being of an immeasurable number of people and families. Traditional legal responses have sought to protect victims through a range of supports and protective measures including the removal of the abuser from the often shared residence. However, by its very nature, domestic abuse typically occurs in a private home environment, one that is often not easily accessed. This article identifies the merits of state intervention measures which seek to challenge the perpetrator, seeking behavioural change through engagement and direction".

I am fully aware of the fact that both males and females are capable of committing acts of domestic violence, but this book is focused on women who are the victim of abuse perpetrated by men. Research on this subject reveals the reality that "most offences are committed by men against women, reflecting the worst manifestation of the gender power imbalance in many intimate relationships. Given that research demonstrates that women in abusive relationships often stay with their abusive partner (Rhodes and Baranoff McKenzie, 1998: 391–2; Gelles, 1974; 1976), adequate protection of such victims mandates that greater efforts are made to eliminate the abuse, insofar as is possible, in order to offer more effective protection. Intervention with perpetrators of domestic violence to effect behavioural change represents an essential element of state efforts to improve the position of victims".

This article considered the capacity and role of the law to direct behavioural change and assessed both international and domestic shifts towards such intervention. This entailed looking at the effective approaches to perpetrator programmes and what could be learned from the UK experience. The article continues to reveal that "when initially introduced in the late 1980s, the UK perpetrator programmes relied upon the US-based Duluth model, premised upon a coordinated community response, designed not to replace the existing criminal justice interventions, but to incorporate targeted intervention to address continued patterns of male violence (Pence and Paymar, 1986).

Whilst originally delivered to both self-referred and court-mandated violent men, the need for accountability for non-compliance resulted in a shift towards court engagement with the probation and prison services, and the development of the Integrated Domestic Abuse Programme (IDAP). The capacity of the courts to monitor a perpetrator's compliance with attendance and participation requirements was identified as a valuable component of this approach (Burton, 2006), whilst also ensuring capacity to track the impact of the intervention through data relating to repeat incidents by those referred".

Two domestic violence interventions delivered by the National Probation Service were the IDAP and the Community Domestic Violence Programme (CDVP). Although delivered by the Ministry of Justice, and distinctive in their respective approaches, the two programmes emphasise an inter-agency approach, working with domestic violence offenders both individually and in group sessions, whilst maintaining strong connections with specialist women's services. Bloomfield and Dixon (2015) evaluated the effectiveness of the two approaches by assessing the re-offending rates in three distinct categories: any offence, any core violence and any domestic violence. Whilst they reported that both programmes were successful in reducing domestic violence re-offences in the two-year follow-up period, it ultimately acknowledges that whilst "the results are promising, many men undergoing treatment went on to reoffend".

Project Mirabel conducted a multisite longitudinal study to assess the impact of non-court mandated community-based perpetrator programmes with a view to understanding *inter alia* whether such programmes work in reducing violence and abuse inflicted by men (Kelly and Westmarland, 2015). A novel element of the findings arises from the extension of measures of success beyond the fact of reduced re-offending, assessed by interviews with relevant parties through the prism of the following measures of success:

• An improved relationship between men on programmes and their partners/ex-partners, which is underpinned by respect and effective communication.

• For partners/ex-partners to have an expanded "space for action", which empowers them by restoring their voice and ability to make choices while improving their well-being.

• Safety and freedom from violence and abuse for women and children.

• Safe, positive and shared parenting.

• Enhanced awareness of self and others for men on programmes, including an understanding of the impact that domestic violence has had on their partner and children.

• Safer, healthier childhoods for children in which they feel heard and cared about (Westmarland et al., 2010: 16).

Thus, success was identified in a more holistic manner, seeking to better and more thoroughly understand the impact, if any, on the behaviour of the perpetrator, the safety of the woman, as well as any improvement in the woman's capacity and ability to assert herself. The final report of the Mirabel Project found that both the "quantitative and qualitative data showed steps toward change for the vast majority of men attending DVPPs". The critical findings were compelling in measuring the impact of the perpetrators' engagement with DVPPs (domestic violence perpetrator programmes), with the research findings determining that "physical and sexual violence was not just reduced but ended for the majority of women in this research". It is important to note that both studies reported an improvement in perpetrator behaviour post-intervention, leading to an improvement in the safety and well-being of their partners.

This outcome indicates that the vast majority of perpetrators stop their physical and sexual violence if they attend a domestic violence perpetrator programme and commit to it from the beginning to the end. The research, led by Durham and London Metropolitan universities, suggests that DVPPs could play an important role in the quest to end domestic violence. DVPPs are good programmes for men to change their behaviour in order to increase the safety of women and children. The programmes in the study above were community-based, meaning that men were not mandated by a criminal court to attend.

The study, which is the first of its kind in the UK, found that before attending the programme, one-third of men made women do something sexual that they did not want to do, but none did so after taking part in the programme (30% to zero). In the same way, cases of the men using a weapon against their partner reduced from 29% to zero. Far fewer women reported being physically injured after the programme, with 61% reporting being physically injured before compared to 2% after. Over half of the women reported feeling "very safe" after the programme, compared to less than one in ten before the programme (51% compared to 8%). However, improvements in the men's coercive and controlling behaviour were weaker, with control of money changing only marginally.

I cannot put enough emphasis on perpetrators seeking support to address the presenting problem. By so doing, their positive actions would help curb violence against women and girls and prevent perpetrators from becoming repeat offenders and continuing this cycle. This research provides valuable insights into the effectiveness of domestic violence perpetrator programmes, depending on where the couple lives. Additionally, the study proves that DVPPs are effective in preventing the repeat offending behaviour as perpetrators are supported to confront their violent and criminal behaviour towards women and children.

CHAPTER 4
Overcoming Abusive Inclinations

It is not uncommon nowadays to recognise that many people are abusive. Whilst no one ever plans to become abusive, it can happen anyway for some of the reasons mentioned in the previous chapters. The reality of the matter is that it can happen to anyone especially, those who are in an intimate relationship. It often starts when the perpetrator becomes resentful instead of loving and compassionate towards their partner. Once they develop a sense of entitlement over their partner, there is always an accompanying feeling of anger and resentment when things do not go according to their vindictive plans or when their actions are challenged by their partner. They want to control everything and think that they have the right to suppress and dominate everyone in their path, especially their partner. Hence, they feel that their partner is obligated to make them feel good or serve them, and if they do not, then they make their partner's life miserable.

The resentment perpetrators feel on the inside is reflected in their misguided attempts to transfer or make others feel the same pain of their failure to lead a meaningful and purposeful life. This causes them to pass the blame for their failures on to those who are closest to them, which in this case is their partner. They feel justified and self-righteous, which comes with anger, threats and violence and makes the perpetrator feel more powerful than their victim. What they might be oblivious to is that such power only makes them monstrous to others. While this gives perpetrators the sense of power they so desire, they are gradually causing damage, as well as destroying intimacy and what may have been a good relationship with their partner.

The problem is that perpetrators never take any responsibility for their actions, and the majority of those who theoretically say they do hardly ever mean it, unless they are ready to make positive changes in their behaviour. Theory without practice is meaningless, and this is where cunningness comes in as they know how to say the right things in the public eye but do the opposite behind closed doors. Until there is an acknowledgement of the problem, there will be no change of heart and therefore no change of habits and actions.

In most cases, perpetrators do not practice what they preach. Instead, they live in self-deceit, portraying themselves as innocent, warm, kind, loving and caring to those outside the relationship. In reality, they are the complete opposite towards their intimate partner. Without knowing it, this forms a character in them and grows into full-fledged pride, selfishness and self-centeredness. Some abusers live in denial all their lives and they are very quick to blame their abusive behaviour on their partner.

Taking accountability and responsibility for the abuse is what differentiates those who are ready for a change to those who want to remain in self-deceit. In its simplicity, this means that after doing some introspection and reflection on their behaviour and conduct, perpetrators admit that they are the cause of pain and distress on their partners and the children involved in these relationships. This pain takes its toll on others in different forms, as previously discussed, whether that's emotionally, physically, mentally, socially or otherwise. It takes sensibility to do this, and any abuser can choose to be "that man" who takes the first step in the right direction for his own benefit and for the benefit of those who are close or connected to him.

Once this step is taken, perpetrators are able to move on to the next stage where they realise that nobody and no circumstance can be held responsible for their behaviour but themselves. Everyone is responsible for their own actions, no matter how they try to justify and cover up their acts. In this case, that includes blaming it on their spouse and other factors, like mental health, alcohol, unemployment, etc. I have to put an emphasis that there is no justification for abuse and for causing pain on others, except for selfishness and wickedness. Whatever reasons or excuses perpetrators may come up with, they can never be justified. They only show weakness instead of their craving for strength and dominance over others.

When a person has been abusive for a long time, they lack skills in different areas of their lives, especially listening to their partner. It often happens that abusers who claim to be listeners do not even understand what listening to someone means. Their listening skills come with self-defence, self-protection, minimisation and denial of the detrimental impact of their actions on their partner. They play mind games and portray their partner as crazy and often claim they are exaggerating the facts being presented to them.

Abusers usually do this to create a camouflage because they have something to hide, i.e., affairs, sexual misconduct, domestic violence or other immoral activities. They provoke an extreme emotional response from their partner so that friends, family and community members believe that their partner is "unstable" or "crazy". Like all types of abuse, mind games can take different forms, including fabricating lies about the partner to ruin their reputation, stalking, intimidation, incrimination and malevolent gossip and accusation. This form of abuse is passive in order to disguise other forms of abuse. Abusers sometimes pretend that they did not hear or understand what their partner has said or claim that she does not make sense.

Pretending that their partner is crazy and hard to deal with can also be a way of gaining sympathy from their friends, or abusers may be simply trying to hide their shame about their failures and lack of success in life. Instead of admitting responsibility or guilt for their failings, they always try to put the blame on their partner. This form of abuse is also used to prevent the partner from leaving due to the fear of desertion and the abuser's dependency on the partner and inability to meet his own needs independently.

One example of this abuse is when abusers share stories of their ex-partners who were never attractive or intellectually up to the abuser's standards, even though he compromised and got into a relationship because of one reason or the other. They explain how they were pursued by women and express empathy for some of their ex-partners who regret leaving them (abusers). These conversations get to the extent of derogatory and disparaging remarks being made about these ex-partners. However, this soon switches to praising their ex-partners for how wonderful they were, and the comparison being made of how "their exes would never do such and such or never act like the current partner", forgetting all the nasty remarks they made earlier about the same ex-partners.

Abusers soon forget about the negativity they portrayed with regard to their ex-partners, which they later turn into positive comments in order to hurt their current partner. This is their strategy to get their partner to tolerate their abusive behaviour. They make them feel like there is "something wrong with them", as their ex-partners were so tolerant and understanding. Abusers use mind games is to emphasise how handsome they are, and if the partner does not conform to their abuse, they will often say "I will find a beautiful young woman the minute I step out of the door" or "I will bring a young girl (meaning younger than the partner) and sleep with her in your bed in your presence". Some curse their wives to death and say, "if you die, I will move on and find someone to marry the next day". These are some of the typical examples of what women go through in their abusive relationships. As hard as this may be to believe, in cases where the partner does sadly pass away, for whatever reason, the abuser does exactly what he said and "'moves on with another woman without thinking twice".

I find it very strange that abusers can come across as more sensitive than the partner they abuse and are quick to react, particularly when the other party expresses their feelings and emotions about the abuse. They view this as an accusation or attack and often respond by making counter-allegations or counteract what is being put on the table for discussion. "Playing the victim" is their favourite phrase—one they use frequently to demoralise their spouse. In reality, they are the one playing the victim. Those who choose to listen instead of reacting immediately in their own defence take on board what is being said and try to understand and make sense out of it. No matter how hard this may be, they reap positive results in the end.

Fear of shame and social stigma are powerful emotional forces that can prevent people from holding themselves accountable and responsible for their immoral behaviours. The same applies to perpetrators of abuse. They do not want to admit their wrongdoing by inflicting pain on their partner as they do not want to be labelled as "abusive" or an "abuser" when in reality, they are abusive. This reminds me of the saying "Hurt people hurt people", and this is especially true when it comes to abuse because most abusers have deep-rooted emotional and psychological burdens that they carry with them. Instead of facing the problem and addressing it, thereby taking the burden off their shoulders, they continue to hurt innocent lives.

My advice would be for perpetrators to break the cycle of abuse by altering their behaviour and lifestyle. This is possible and achievable for those who seek support in addressing this problematic behaviour. Learning to manage one's emotions early is essential, and it goes a long way towards attaining a healthy and satisfying relationship with one's partner and the family at large. Below, I list a few suggestions about abusive trends that have to be overcome and share tips on things perpetrators can do to become a better person/partner:

1. Stop being selfish

I cannot emphasise enough that selfishness is the primary root of domestic abuse. Although perpetrators of this evil do not always see themselves as "selfish", they truly are. Think about this: why do perpetrators think someone else has to suffer because that person did not please them? Do they think it is fair to be insulted, name called, accused, physically and mentally hurt, raped, and sadly killed just because their partner does not agree or see eye to eye with them about something? People are different and unique. Therefore, their thinking process and perception also differs from others. Just because the perpetrator wants everything done in their own way and according to their own knowledge and terms does not mean that only their style is correct and their partner's ways of doing things are wrong. This attitude only wants to "feed themself" to be satisfied, without considering if others are alright or not.

The attitude of selfishness occurs because the perpetrator has become so self-absorbed. They do not care about the needs or feelings of their partner or how their abuse is affecting them. It is only about the perpetrator and nothing else. The failure to accommodate other people's errors or to make a compromise in consideration of another person is selfishness. Abusers' conversations are about themselves. It's "I, myself and me", and most of the time, they get into relationships because they are looking to gain something. They basically want their needs to be met without bringing anything valuable into the relationship.

Many perpetrators are dependent on the same women they abuse for their basic needs to be met. The women in these relationships become miserable because they have to spend their lives giving and never receiving anything back, except criticism and dissatisfaction, no matter how selfless they are towards the abuser. Perpetrators are never satisfied, and they are never grateful for what has been done for them. They just want more and more. Their glass is always half empty, they are very pessimistic about the affairs of life, and they are extremely hard to please.

This creeps in slowly through the factors above, and if any man falls into this category, they are potentially treading the path of abuse. They have to look within themselves and make a conscious effort to make amends. Perpetrators need to re-evaluate themselves and ask themselves why it always has to be them who is the offended party? Does it mean perpetrators are the only ones with feelings and no one else matters? Or does it mean their partner's feelings mean nothing to them? Could this mean that there is something about perpetrators that is problematic and needs to be resolved? They need to identify their selfish traits and work on becoming better men. By so doing, they will lead a joyful and fulfilled life where they will thrive and succeed in all that they and their partner get involved in.

2. Become sensitive to their partner's needs and emotions

Having no sense of empathy towards their partner's needs or emotions is a result of selfishness and self-centeredness, as I mentioned earlier. As a result of this, abusers fail to adopt emotional intelligence and therefore do not recognise their own emotions and those of others. Emotional intelligence is the ability to process one's own and other people's emotions and being able to consider how one's actions make others feel. It is also associated with empathy and compassion towards others, whilst recognising their emotional difficulties and being able to connect with them deeply.

An inability or unwillingness to ever listen and hear their partner's point of view, as well as constantly interrupting them in every conversation, is not pleasant. Perpetrators need to let their partner express themselves and their views without quickly dismissing or never acknowledging them. It goes without saying that conversations with perpetrators always tend to be so overwhelming and dominated by them. These conversations are always centred around *their* needs and feelings, with very little attention (if any at all) paid to their partner's needs. They never ask meaningful questions to genuinely find out how their partner is doing or pay attention to her answers.

Perpetrators need to recognise that the maturity people seek in relationships lies within fair treatment by their spouse, being respected, and being with someone who is sensible and pragmatic when their emotions are running high. This not only calls for physical sensibility, but it requires emotional control from men who have developed a full understanding of their own emotions, as they are able to put themselves in other people's shoes. Perpetrators need to train themselves in this area so they will be able to understand their partner's emotional needs and thereby be able to predict how their partner will feel before they say anything to them. For married couples, knowing what to say, when to say it, and how to say it makes a huge difference between staying married and heading for divorce.

If perpetrators can practice this and be considerate enough to give their partner the necessary dose of attention, love, care and everything else required to make a relationship succeed, then this would be reciprocated by their partner. Once this happens, the cycle continues until the bond becomes stronger and healthier. However, this requires the perpetrator to decide to alter their ways and actions and seek support in their journey to change their narrative. They have to stand up to the task of exterminating their toxic attributes that are harmful to their partner and their loved ones at large. There is support available depending on where one lives, and all it takes is asking for help or talking to someone who can offer guidance.

3. Pay attention to themselves and they will be able to pay attention to their partner

When having a conversation with their partner, perpetrators have to pay attention to be able to understand her. Since discussions are a way of communicating feelings, perpetrators will learn and know how best to respond to her feelings as she expresses them. Abusers are very contemptuous in their mannerisms and quickly jump into making negative judgements without ever fully listening to their partner's feelings. Their prejudice makes them incapable of viewing things from a positive angle, and they often focus on their partner's shortfalls and use these to gain more ground for abuse. Once the perpetrator begins to resent their partner, even if they deny this in words, they need to try to look for the partner's good qualities, especially those that attracted them to her in the first place.

If they can pay attention to their partner, then they will be able to respect them. Perpetrators have no sense of respect, and I find it intriguing that they see this as the woman's responsibility, not theirs. This goes back to the influence of cultural backgrounds, which I highlighted earlier, where some men embrace the patriarchal norms in their societies and use these to oppress their partner from every angle. I have come across headstrong perpetrators who believe that "it is the woman's responsibility to study, know, understand and respect a man", whilst the man rules the roost.

Perpetrators fight their corner to ensure that these oppressive beliefs are adhered to by their partner, and if not, they resort to abuse and violence. They have no concept of reciprocity and are consumed by receiving from the partner without ever giving back. Sound men who embrace these simple but yet profound basic skills never demand respect. Instead, they display this towards their partner. This, in turn, gets reciprocated without having to fight for it.

"Do unto others as you would have them do unto you" is the key when it comes to this area of relationships, and it simply means that you should treat your partner the way you would like to be treated. Perpetrators therefore have to learn to respect their partner first and avoid any behaviours that come across as disrespectful towards the partner. They can also take this a step further by learning to ignore any behaviour displayed by their partner that may seem disrespectful towards them. Also, they need to remember that respect means different things to different people, and what one may consider disrespectful may be acceptable and normal elsewhere. Just because perpetrators do not agree with something, does not mean it is wrong, but it means they need to learn to view things from other people's perspectives and listen to their views.

Perpetrators who do not want to be challenged about their immoral behaviour—or who do not want their partner to have a say or express their opinions about the abuse at hand—use this as one of their weapons to wage war against their partner. It is time for perpetrators to change, take a step back, listen to their partner, and take action to address the issues that are presented. Their attention is important and everything else will follow as perpetrators begin to listen to their partner and take their needs and feelings seriously.

4. Stop demanding and controlling their partners

Perpetrators should always remember that a relationship is a two-way street. This means that whatever they or their partner choose to do in the relationship is by choice and mutual agreement between the two, so no one has to hold the other by the throat simply because they are not conforming to their "demands". The first thing perpetrators do is isolate their partner from her friends and family. They do this in a very manipulative, cunning and crafty way that will take their partner longer to notice or realise.

For instance, perpetrators will say they do not have friends, they like to keep to themselves, they do not like to interfere in other people's business, and this includes their own family, they do not like visitors or visiting people, etc. Maybe they make negative comments about their friends and associates, thus discouraging any form of communication with them and always find something terribly negative to say about them. Or they try to turn their partner against anyone they are close to or reliant on for support. Their goal is to strip away their partner's support network and strength so they will not be able to stand up against their abuse as it advances.

Perpetrators feel that they have the right to know more than they actually do. I believe in honesty and openness between all partners involved in any relationship, whether it is a work relationship, friendship or intimate relationship. But perpetrators take this a step further by always demanding that their partner shares everything with them, i.e., if the partner receives a call from someone, the perpetrator will ask "Who was that?", "Why are they phoning you?", "What did they say?", "What did you say?" or "How did you respond to...?" Sometimes one does things without keeping any record, without violating any boundaries, and maybe for the benefit of the relationship.

It is therefore not right to question every action the partner takes. This is what leads to depression and anxiety as the partner has to be conscious of everything they say or do and has to account for every minute of their whereabouts every day. It becomes painful when women are made to feel like they are walking on eggshells. Perhaps the perpetrator constantly checks their partner's phone, emails, internet history, etc. Their justification for this is that they have been cheated on previously and have developed trust issues. Well, they tell the same story to all their chain of partners. This has nothing to do with the partner. It is simply one of the traits of abuse and inferiority commonly exhibited by perpetrators.

It is also common for perpetrators to be jealous, and this comes with accusations and paranoia (a mental condition characterised by delusions of persecution, unwarranted jealousy, or exaggerated self-importance, typically worked into an organised system that leads to unjustified suspicion and mistrust of other people). It's sad to say that most perpetrators exhibit this behaviour, but they never acknowledge it. They initially display this as charming or as a sign of how much they care or how attached they are to their partner. This is nothing more than disguised insecurity, and it soon turns into excessive control and paranoia.

Research has shown that abusers tend to be very demanding as a result of their sense of entitlement, pride and self-centeredness. Since they think they are better than their partner, they demand that their partner pleases them at all costs. In fact, the partner is often stripped of her sense of self and identity, as her life "should" revolve around the abusive partner's needs. Needless to say, the worst partners are those who feel entitled to their partner's possessions by claiming "rights of ownership" simply by association, not even acknowledging their partner's diligence in attaining what the abuser find himself enjoying.

Perpetrators can suddenly become violent when their partner attempts to set boundaries and make the abuser understand that they have exclusive rights to their own assets. For instance, some women earn more than their spouse and are supporting him financially and otherwise. Instead of being appreciative and grateful for the support and the good life they never worked for, the abuser feels inferior, obsessive and materialistic and wants to control everything. Should the woman reach a point of withdrawing the privileges, the abuser wages a war against her in retaliation. The abuser can become hostile and violent and can be quick to pull the victim card in the process.

It should be pointed out that abusers of this category are the laziest men who act like parasites and do not want to work. They are the ones who sit on the couch or bed all day watching TV and have knowledge about all the latest films and TV programmes. They are the ones who have time to peruse their partner's personal information and turn everything they find against them. These are the vindictive, spiteful and manipulative abusers who intentionally plan evil against their partner.

They propagate hatred and malice against their partner in order to isolate them even further so they will be able to hide their evil acts in the long run. These perpetrators live in hypocrisy and would curse and threaten their partner with evil to the point of cursing them with "death" if they do not commit murder themselves as they have time to envision and plan this evil. I repeat, it is time that perpetrators stop and think realistically about their character and state of mind. They can still make suitable changes that will be beneficial, not only to their spouse but to themselves in future.

5. Understand that violence is not the root of their problem

Perpetrators have to understand that their violent behaviour is the result of their resentment towards their partner, which manifests itself in the form of the abusive tendencies that we earlier discussed. It does not start with violence; it starts with their heart and mindset. The fact is that the perpetrator's problem starts a long time before violence comes into the picture. This might have been as a result of violence that they experienced in their childhood or as a result of toxic ideologies that they picked up when they were growing up. As a result of these experiences, perpetrators might have made some wrong decisions and acquired harmful habits that now contribute to their abusive behaviour. Although the past is understandable and may have caused deep, unaddressed wounds that need attention in order to heal, their acts of abuse and violence are not justifiable.

Once perpetrators realise that there is something wrong with "them" and not with their partner, they should reflect and pinpoint the experiences that created the person they have become. Whenever they get to the point of lashing out against their partner, they should remind themselves that "she is not the cause of their problem". The partner is not the reason for the perpetrator's emptiness, bitterness and contempt, and if they are wise enough to see this, the partner could actually be the one to bring healing to the perpetrator's hurt. If the perpetrator is not able to come to terms with these facts, they will continue to live in denial of their own problems, and they will keep pointing their finger at the innocent women they meet, blaming each woman they form a relationship with for their own unaddressed problems.

6. Perpetrators should curb their pride

This is one of the common causes of abuse in relationships. When a relationship is not birthed by love, but for selfish reasons, pride creeps in within no time. Men are quick to assume the superior role due to patriarchal beliefs, and whilst there may be nothing wrong with this in healthy relationships, abusers use this to their advantage. So, they demand that their partner be submissive to them, especially the ones with narcissistic tendencies. According to research, narcissists have an exaggerated sense of self-worth, so they are always manipulative and controlling as they target their partner's self-esteem. Once they can break their partner's self-esteem, they begin to manipulate and control them.

A bible verse "Wives, submit to your husband" followed by a brief statement about how "the husband is the head of the wife just as Christ is the head of the church" is known and mostly used by every abusive man in religious settings. This is one of their favourite verses used oppressively and unjustly to cover their malevolent acts when their partner challenges or does not conform to their abusive behaviour. What they miss is the latter part of the scripture that admonishes men to love their wives as Christ loves the church. Men who genuinely love their wives do not have to preach sermons on submission to them, but this automatically falls in place as a result of the love and warmth they exude towards their wives. No woman should submit to an abusive and disdainful man who is consumed by egocentric demands and pride.

Getting caught up in their own ideas does keep perpetrators from listening to their partner's ideas, which then means they cannot see things from their partner's perspective. Instead, they act as though their thoughts and feelings are the only ones that matter. Additionally, they do not want to listen to others or ask for help, as they assume, they know everything and no one can tell them anything. Unfortunately, this leads them to ignore and reject the things that could be beneficial for them solely because they were suggested or came from their partner. Because they think they know everything, they do not want to acknowledge when someone else has a better idea and often resort to fighting and criticising the idea being presented. This shows how immature abusers are and how little respect they have for others. It also ultimately alienates them from positive social networks. Remember that "pride goes before a fall", and their relationships do fall whilst they are consumed with pride.

7. Put an end to persistent disparagement

Criticism is something that can start small but can actually cause hurt in the relationship. Abusers like to frame this as though they are trying to make their partner better. They often emphasise this by saying, "I am trying to make your life better". By doing so, they are trying to get the partner to trivialise the seriousness of the problem. Women with an abusive partner are subject to a lot of criticism by virtue of constantly going through natural physical and hormonal changes as they grow. This extends from criticism of physiological changes to their lifestyle choices, preferences and interests.

The bigger problem is that due to domestic abuse/violence, many relationships/marriages break down. Therefore, some partners move on and meet someone else when they are advanced in age and have lived their lives in certain ways that are suitable and comfortable for them. So, when these two individuals come together, there is a need for adjustments and compromise on both sides in order to make the relationship work successfully.

This is where abusive men exhibit high levels of control as they want to turn their partner into robot clones, wanting them to change their lifestyle completely to suit the abuser's style of living. They become so critical of the way their partner speaks, dresses, cooks, eats, decorates their house, the car they drive and, remarkably, they often even undermine their career, shrewdly convincing them to leave their job. Eventually, it seems that everything the partner does, the abuser is never satisfied with. They are always looking for something negative to criticise instead of commending what has been accomplished.

It is great when partners can challenge each other in interesting discussions, as this allows them to try new ways of thinking about or viewing the matters at hand. But it is terrible when they make their partner feel small, stupid, or they consistently try to change their mind about something important to them or every idea they air out. Openness to new ideas and experiences is wonderful, but a controlling partner never sees this as a two-way street. It is always a one-way street in their minds.

Belittling their partner and making them feel worthless, unattractive, or as if they do not "measure up" is the ultimate goal of abusers. They do this by subtly and constantly emphasising their professional accomplishments compared to their partner's accomplishments or experience. I have come across terrible stories where abusers would even constantly and unfavourably compare their current partner with their ex-partners. Everything their partner does would be compared to the ex-partner/s, which raises the question of why their previous relationships ended if their ex-partners were so great. This unfortunately extends to the intimate part of the relationship, crushing any emotions and affection that once were genuine and selfless.

It creates a toxic environment where one party has to work harder to please someone who is not and never will be satisfied or pleased by anything. This is just part of their dominant behaviour in the relationship. The abuser makes their partner feel mentally drained so they will eventually give in to the abuse, allowing them to then fully exert their influence over them. This is common when the partner, by virtue of their cultural or religious beliefs, is more submissive to male dominance. As a result, the abuser triumphs in every disagreement that arises. In other cases, it may be that the partner is more conflict-avoidant in nature or is simply exhausted from the battle they are in with their abuser, who has seemingly been successful in using disparaging tools to weaken their partner's resolve.

It takes sensibility and determination to adjust and make changes to the things that people are accustomed to. Perpetrators can also change this attitude with time. They need to keep in mind that whilst they may have legitimate concerns that need to be discussed with their partner, anger and criticism does not help the situation. The perpetrator's concerns can get lost because criticism often triggers a defence response from the partner, which leads to disputes and frustration with no resolution to the problem at hand. Communication has to done be in a

way that focuses on understanding and addressing the
issue, rather than trying to attack or hurt their partner.

CHAPTER 5
Understanding manhood and its responsibilities

In the previous chapter, we discussed the need to overcome the noxious ideologies that contribute to men's abusive behaviour and the necessary steps to help change this. Vocabulary Dictionary describes "manhood" as both the adult period in a male human's life and the qualities that make him a man. Whilst some people believe that a boy reaches manhood when he hits puberty, others maintain that manhood is based on becoming independent and responsible. I agree with both, particularly the latter part of this description. A real man protects his partner physically, emotionally and in other different ways. His love for his partner is unconditional, and he provides her with financial security and comfort, makes her feel safe and secure, and is never abusive in any form.

Unfortunately, society has made men believe that their male power is only reflected when they do not show emotions or when they show physical strength, stubbornness and hardness. These ideas were birthed by patriarchy, misogyny and sexism. Men do have emotions, but society has taught them to "man up" by not showing these emotions. Expressing their emotions does not mean they are weak. However, depending on the part of the world they live in, some men are trained to suppress their emotions. Consequently, they express them in an abusive and violent way. No wonder violence is prevalent and normalised in some parts of the world. This is not a justification for abuse, but it means that men need to learn to express their emotions in a non-abusive manner that will not hurt the person on the receiving end.

Real men do not shift the blame or try to defend their mistakes. They simply acknowledge when they have made a mistake and apologise. This does not make them any less manly; in fact, it demonstrates that they are confident and have the courage and integrity to admit their faults. The fact is that real men are not manufactured. No one is damaged beyond repair and nothing is impossible for those who believe in making changes to their circumstances and general functioning. Even narcissists can find redemption if they set their minds to it.

Being a better man and behaving as such has to start from within, and for those who wish to transform their behaviour and their life, I have added a few tips below:

• Respect your partner for who she is

Real men love their spouses for who they are and not for what she possesses or her status. There may be times when a couple does not see eye to eye, but real men love their spouse anyway, and this love is not subject to conditions. The focus is not only on the partner's outward beauty but on her personality and everything that lies within the partner. Real men know that nature takes its course on the body as time goes by. Rather than trying to bring them down to make themselves feel good, they treat their partner with respect and dignity. The opposite is true for the abusers. Instead of cherishing and adoring their partner for who she is, they make all kinds of nasty comments and become really sarcastic towards her.

A sense of humour and even teasing can be a fundamental mode of interacting within many long-term relationships. The key aspect is whether it feels comfortable and loving to both parties. In many controlling relationships, abusers use this as one of their weapons to attack their partner, and after making nasty comments, they say "I was just joking". Knowingly or unknowingly, the abuser keeps repeating the same nasty comments or criticisms about the same issue. However, they then turn the tables around once there is a reaction from the partner and blame her for having the wrong reaction to his joke. Most abusers even deny the cynical comments they throw at their partner and portray their partner as having a problem with their cognitive ability particularly if she repeats the nasty remarks made by the abuser.

Often times, abusers have a way of planting seeds of doubt about their partner's talents and aspirations, making them feel they are not good enough. This is one of the ways they take away their partner's autonomy, so they will become indebted to them. They ruin professional or educational goals by making their partner doubt herself and give up on her dreams. It amazes me how the same people who have never tried or attempted to achieve anything positive in life tend to be the ones who claim to "know everything". Abusers are specialists in this field. They are experts in making their partner believe that her ideas are ridiculous and can never come to fruition.

This eventually leads to loss of confidence and optimism on the partner's side. A supportive man would take a different approach to this and would respect and support his partner's visions and ideas.

• Take responsibility for your shortcomings and errors

In healthy relationships, when men have caused pain or harm to their partner, they acknowledge and own what they have done and take responsibility for it. This is followed by taking steps to never repeat the same blunder and changing their behaviours with the aim of developing greater levels of love, care, empathy and respect for their partner. The man does whatever it takes to try to hear, understand and empathise with their partner and therefore takes the responsibility required to stop blaming their partner for everything that goes wrong. In abusive relationships, men are motivated to be right and get their way at all costs and maintain control over their spouse. They unknowingly relinquish personal responsibility for their harmful words and actions and deny any wrongdoing, with some boldly claiming to be right all the time.

Men who use coercive control against their partner deny their abusive behaviour completely, but they can contradict themselves sometimes. They occasionally admit to causing harm but dismiss it, saying the abuse was not that bad or convincing their partner that their relationship is the best she could hope for. This is part of abuser's coercive control, and it is applied with rationality and reasoning by reminding the partner of times they were right, and she was wrong. When given feedback about their abusive behaviour, they are good at diverting the attention away from themselves and pull their partner's personality apart. Moreover, abusers always find one reason or another to justify their behaviour, i.e., stress, health, alcohol, unemployment and anything or anyone else, or by distorting things so that it appears the partner is somehow responsible.

People make mistakes, but when these mistakes are blamed on others, it shows that there is no hope for change on the blaming side. In abusive relationships, this shows that the abuser is not taking personal responsibility and accountability for their behaviour. These control tactics are the hallmarks of relationships that never become as loving, caring or healthy as the abused partner had hoped for. It is time that abusers understand that their errors are the results of their thoughts, actions and decisions, and that they need to take responsibility for them and cease blaming anyone else for their immoral actions.

• **Protect your partner instead of causing her harm**

Men and women are wired differently by nature and society. Women are emotionally sensitive and like to be cherished and feel safe and secure in their relationship/marriage. In some societies, women are financially dependent on their spouses, and as long as the man can provide financial stability for them, then everything is fine. What men do not understand is that it is not only financial stability that women need. They also need to feel protected and valued, and in turn, she will automatically reciprocate in kind and go the extra mile in her kindness. Perhaps the biggest part of emotional protection is protecting the marriage/relationship.

It is intriguing to know that most abusers have no mental filter and they destroy their own relationships by virtue of their vindictiveness. Instead of protecting the marriage from external forces or intruders, abusers are the ones who open the door for destruction. This is due to their failure to recognise that the problem lies within them, not with the partner. I have come across abusers who truly believe that their partner is not smart enough, has a low IQ level compared to the abuser and is not beautiful enough. It just seems that they are never enough in the mind of the abuser. This is what constitutes an unhealthy relationship that ends in disaster.

Instead of being warm, loving and kind towards their partner, the abuser often deliberately frustrates or provokes their partner to trigger anger or extreme emotion. After a prolonged period of abuse, and when their partner has started to react to this behaviour, the abuser does this to provoke a reaction. By so doing, abusers derive pleasure from watching their partner become distressed and react to the abuse. Whatever the logic behind this behaviour is, it is mainly used as a tactic to dominate or control their spouse. Once the abuser gets a reaction from their partner, the abuser then uses this against her to prove to others that she is the problem in the relationship, not them.

Abusers conceal their actions and only capture the response they get from their partner. Some go as far as taking pictures, voice recordings and videos claiming to be the evidence of how uncooperative, easily angered, mentally unstable, provocative their partner is. Some are even brave enough to claim their partner is aggressive. Abusers become even angrier and think that their rage is justified, blame their partner for being "provocative" and claim they are "just defending themselves". They seem to possess special skills in counteracting and making counter-allegations against their partner, and it takes wise and trained people to understand the general functioning of abusers.

By blaming their partner for the argument, the attention is diverted away from abuser's own behaviour. They ensure that their partner is left confused and hurt so they will be easily manipulated. Once an abuser identifies kindness, they use this as a weapon to exploit their partner. It seems that abusers enjoy the sense of power and control they derive from taunting their partner and this is exacerbated by the positive attention they receive from their associates or allies. Moreover, abusers use this strategy to exhaust their partner emotionally and mentally so they will become compliant with the abusive behaviour and avoid the dreadful consequences should they not conform. This is common when the partner has become resistant to the abuse or when they have learned to combat the abuse.

A decent man will protect his wife. He will not do anything that will cause her hurt or harm. Men like this choose their words wisely, avoid any negativity that will impact on their partner's emotional wellbeing and avoid making their relationship unhealthy. They stand up for their partner and back them up when under attack from family members, friends and associates. Abusers are good at badmouthing their partner, and they let the enemy come into their relationship to cause distraction. They allow the outsiders to crush their partner, causing even more damage to the relationship. Surprisingly, some abusers like affection and enjoy actions of fondness from their partner, but sadly, they are selfish enough to not think of reciprocating the same affection. They only want for them is to be on the receiving end and never give back.

- **Be a leader, not a dominator**

Showing good leadership skills in a relationship is really about demonstrating capability—for example, a man's ability to listen and actually hear what is being said; the ability to empathise with the partner; showing appropriate skills in dealing with conflict and willingness to be fully accountable for his own actions and attitude. It also means that as a good leader in the relationship, a man should not always blame their partner nor avert from accountability. People often talk about who "wears the trousers" in a relationship and there are a lot of jokes about wives "bossing" around their husbands—but the truth is, in order for a relationship to flourish, there needs to be good leadership in it, not authoritarian, inflexible, demanding and oppressive leadership.

Being a leader does not mean carrying the weight of the whole world on your shoulders. It simply means that a man rises up to take charge of situations when necessary. People have a certain level of respect and admiration for those who can handle difficult situations without becoming aggressive or abusive. Leadership means bringing out the best in the team, taking full accountability for errors and inaccuracies, and giving full credit for successes to those they lead. This style of leadership applies equally to marriages and relationships. No woman wants to get into a relationship with someone who withdraws and takes the back seat when their attention is needed to solve problems or who resorts to violence when challenging situations occur.

Leadership requires strength. And this has nothing to do with physical strength. It's about mental and emotional strength, where a man is able to keep his feelings in check and control his passions. When he is angry, he does not act out of his emotions by resorting to physical abuse. Masculinity encompasses many positive qualities, i.e., decision-making abilities, decisiveness, strength, confidence, discipline, integrity, accountability, honesty, self-reliance etc. These are some of the attributes of a good leader and a determining factor in how a man will take the lead role in the relationship. It takes strength to be able to suppress one's anger. It does not mean that a man is timid. In fact, it reflects strength and integrity.

Arguments, disagreements, and conflicts are not only inevitable in some relationships, but when handled in a positive manner and with maturity, they do not have a devastating impact and outcome on those relationships. A man should share his thoughts and feelings with his partner without reservations, discuss difficult subject matters, and can disagree with her, yet he can still come to some kind of resolution without being aggressive or abusive towards his partner. Many couples communicate in a destructive way that leads to frustration, anger and disconnection, whereas others avoid having meaningful discussions to avoid fights.

Either way is not good. There needs to be a balance and clear middle ground for both parties to thrive in their relationship.

A responsible and emotionally intelligent man who can control his impulses shows true maturity. As such, he likely has the capacity to deal with the change, disappointment, stress and conflict that life and relationships bring. This is a well-grounded man with a sense of balance who can confront life in a constructive way while remaining a resilient, supportive and engaging of his partner in the process. The opposite is true for abusive men who respond to challenging issues irresponsibly, react impulsively and abusively to the challenges but then direct these negative responses towards their partner. Sound men do not dominate. They lead by example in their families, especially in their relationships with their spouses and embrace the saying, "Practice what you preach".

What needs to be done next

Once abusers have been able to identify the reasons why they are abusive and how to curb these tendencies, as already discussed in the previous chapters, they have to find techniques to help them get rid of this toxic behaviour completely. Abusive men often have an underlying attitude, which is something exceedingly difficult to change as they do not see anything wrong with their actions. Apologising and temporarily acting "nice" again are not true indications of change. The real change takes time and a tremendous amount of effort and commitment to achieve. It is not enough for abusers to know that they are selfish or controlling and only understanding the reasons "why". They need to think deeper and not rush through the process of rediscovering themselves in order to walk the path of restoration meaningfully.

Dealing with reality is much better than sugar-coating the problem. This means taking huge responsibility for positive life changes. Therefore, there is a need for abusers to adopt some strategies to cope with these changes, especially where there is some consideration of professional intervention. Since the abuser's partner has been hurt by the toxicity of the relationship, while seeking support to address the problem, the abuser needs to stay away from the partner and vice versa until such time that the process is complete. Where there is still hope for the relationship to be maintained and not much damage has been caused, the abuser can still involve their partner in the healing process despite staying apart. They should let their partner know the effort being made in the transformation of their behaviour. Depending on the circumstances between the parties, this works quite well for some couples and it helps in the healing of the relationship.

This can also be applied on a daily basis when emotions run high. The abuser can take himself away from the partner by going for a walk until he has calmed down and is in a better place to talk about the issue instead of exploding in anger. The process of genuinely changing harmful/abusive behaviour is long, slow and difficult. It takes a lifetime to learn abusive behaviour, so unlearning such behaviour, while completely possible, also takes a lot of time and committed work in intervention programmes specifically designed to help abusive men recognise their abuse patterns and learn new, healthy patterns. Additionally, abusers who really want to change will also have to address other underlying problems, such as mental health, alcoholism, drug misuse, etc.

The thought and promise of change can fill both partners with hope that maybe things will get better. Hope is a beautiful thing and wanting a relationship to get better is not foolish or shameful. It is a testament to the abuser's optimism and resilience. Sadly, without serious intervention, no matter what the abuser promises, the cycle of abuse continues. That is why it is important to focus not only on what the abuser says but on what they do. When abusers continue to put themselves first, blame their partner or put them down, unfortunately, their promises to change are just a way to maintain control. The first sign of a real commitment is when abusers stop focusing on themselves, start feeling true empathy for their partner, and genuinely recognise the harm that they have caused to them.

Sometimes abusers and controlling men genuinely want to change for a number of reasons, such as regretting having hurt their loved ones, having had enough of being angry, being tired of feeling alone and misunderstood, and being tired of monitoring another person, etc. They may also be exhausted by their own possessiveness and covetousness or they may remember a controlling person they never want to resemble, i.e., fathers or other male figures in their childhood. Abusers who dare take these difficult steps towards making changes report feeling happier and more at peace once this behaviour is addressed. Their relationships feel stronger and more genuine, their children are no longer afraid of them, and they also enjoy better friendships where they can truly connect with others in their spheres of contact.

CHAPTER 6
Effects of Domestic Abuse/Violence on the Abused Partner

As established in previous chapters, abuse can take on different forms, and there are none in the list that are without negative effects on the abused partner. Women who have been in abusive relationships face a lot of traumatic effects, ranging from physical to psychological impacts. While there may be scars from physical abuse, unseen scars are the most incomprehensible ones as they cut deep into their emotional and mental wellbeing.

An article in *Women's Health* in January of 2019 states, "If you have experienced a physical or sexual assault, you may feel many emotions—fear, confusion, anger, or even being numb and not feeling much of anything. You may feel guilt or shame over being assaulted. Some people try to minimise the abuse or hide it by covering bruises and making excuses for the abuser. If you have been physically or sexually assaulted or abused, know that it is not your fault. Getting help for assault or abuse can help prevent long-term mental health effects and other health problems".

Long-term mental health effects of violence against women can include:

•   Post-traumatic stress disorder (PTSD).

This can be a result of experiencing trauma or having a shocking or terrifying experience, such as sexual assault or physical abuse. Abused partners may easily feel shocked, anxious, have difficulty sleeping and may have anger outbursts. It is also important to mention that, amongst other things, they may have trouble remembering things or may develop negative thoughts about themselves or others. Abused partners live in fear and uncertainty as they are unable to predict when the next attack will come. Once they become isolated from family and friends, they become completely reliant and dependent on the abuser. The abuser will often use this against their partner to prove their so-called "innocence" about the abuse if they happen to remain in the picture.

PTSD can cause some people to react to fear in the form of emotional and behavioural signs, whilst in others, it manifests itself in the form of dysphoric mood swings or dissociative signs. Dysphoria is a profound sense of unease or dissatisfaction. While it is not a mental health diagnosis on its own, it is a symptom associated with a variety of mental illnesses, such as anxiety, depression, and substance use disorders. Typically, PTSD is caused by the overreaction of stress hormones, so the abused partner begins to experience the fight, flight or freeze reaction. As a result, it becomes impossible for them to maintain focus.

Although the reason for the brain getting stuck in short-term memories is to protect the abused partner from danger, it can become discomforting when it starts happening too often, and this leads to them feeling miserable. Often, the events of a distant past will continue to haunt the abused partner as though it is still happening. Eventually, they will start to feel a rush of PTSD symptoms, like anxiety, nightmares, hyper-vigilance, etc. Once the partner starts experiencing symptoms of PTSD, their brain will no longer be effective in processing information because their stress hormones are always overreacting. Everything begins to scare them, so their fight or flight response is always active.

In cases like this, even the most inconsequential incidents make the abused person raise their guard. When they come in contact with anything that challenges them, they instinctively run away because they feel too vulnerable in that environment.

- Depression and Anxiety Disorders

According to *Medical News Today*, published on the 22nd of November 2019, "Depression is a mood disorder that involves a persistent feeling of sadness and loss of interest. It is different from the mood fluctuations that people regularly experience as a part of life". Depression and anxiety disorders are different, but people with depression often experience symptoms similar to those of an anxiety disorder, such as nervousness, irritability, and problems sleeping and concentrating. But each disorder has its own causes and its own emotional and behavioural symptoms. If untreated, depression can become a major problem in one's life. Major depression is characterised by at least five of the diagnostic symptoms, of which at least one of the symptoms is either an overwhelming feeling of sadness or a loss of interest and pleasure in most of their usual activities.

The other symptoms that are associated with major depression include a decrease or increase in appetite, insomnia or hypersomnia, psycho-motor agitation or retardation, constant fatigue, feelings of worthlessness or excessive and inappropriate guilt, recurrent thoughts of death and suicidal ideation with or without specific plans for committing suicide, and cognitive difficulties, such as diminished ability to think, concentrate and make decisions. This impacts the person's overall welfare and social integration, i.e., the person loses motivation for socialisation, pursuing their education or career and other aspects of life. Many people who develop depression have a history of an anxiety disorder earlier in life. There is no evidence that one disorder causes the other, but there is clear evidence that many people suffer from both disorders. Depression is a serious illness, and it is advisable to seek support when one feels these symptoms.

Depression is a profoundly serious illness that many abused partners experience. This is often associated with numbness, a constant feeling of sadness and anxiety. This leads me to conclude that amongst other traumatic life experiences, domestic abuse/violence is near the top of the list. According to experts, violence is equated to a hidden epidemic that can be associated with mental health conditions. Women in abusive relationships are almost two times more prone to depression than those who have not experienced abuse. In addition to the stress that comes from the abuse women face, additional factors might lead to other symptoms of depression in abused partners, so the greater the abuse, the more severe the symptoms of depression. New mothers who are in abusive relationships are said to be two times more prone to postpartum depression than those in normal relationships. Other factors that may contribute to depression among women who are in abusive relationships are genetics, substance misuse, poor physical health, etc. due to the vulnerability these create.

Anxiety is a feeling of unease, such as worry or fear, that can be mild or severe. Everyone experiences some feelings of anxiety at some point in their life, which can be perfectly normal. Some people can be unable to control their feelings of anxiety when they become more constant and impact on their daily lives. Anxiety is the main symptom of several conditions, including a sudden attack of intense fear. Other effects can include shutting people out, not wanting to do things you once enjoyed, not being able to trust others, and having low self-esteem.

Abused partners who have experienced serious physical abuse, concussion and traumatic brain injury (TBI) from being hit on the head or falling and hitting their head can experience the following: Headaches or a feeling of pressure, loss of consciousness, confusion, dizziness, memory loss, trouble concentrating, sleep loss, etc. Some symptoms of TBI may take a few days to show up. Over an extended period, TBI can cause depression and anxiety. TBI can also cause problems with your thoughts, including the ability to make plans and action them. This can make it more difficult for an abused partner to leave an abusive relationship. The short-term physical effects of violence can include minor injuries or serious conditions. They can include bruises, cuts, broken bones, or injuries to organs and other internal parts of the body, which can only be seen through scans or x-rays. It's therefore imperative that the physically abused partner seeks support from the medical professionals to address the problem.

Over time, their self-esteem may be worn down, like water dripping on a stone. They may start to believe their abuser's insults and start blaming themselves for the abuse or deny that it is taking place. They may ignore it, hoping that their abuser will change over time. Abused partners often experience conflicting emotions, such as fear, anger, shame, resentment, sadness and powerlessness. They are not weak, submissive victims but they are courageous and resourceful. It takes huge mental strength to live with an abusive partner and have to adopt all kinds of coping strategies to survive each day. Albeit, they become weary of doing this by themselves, which is why they should seek support professionals or someone they trust who will not judge them and make their circumstances far worse than they already are. Anxiety thrives in the most chaotic situations; thus, abusive relationships are a perfect breeding ground for it, and this continues even after the partner has left the relationship.

- Substance Misuse

Some abused partners resort to taking drugs, drinking alcohol excessively, smoking and overreacting to the challenges and the situations they face. Substance misuse is linked to sexual abuse in several ways. The first one is where the perpetrator uses substances before they commit the act. The second one is where the perpetrator forces the victim to take drugs or alcohol before they engage them in the act. The third is where the victim uses substances to cope with the aftermath of sexual assault or abuse. I would like us to talk about the third one due to its relevance to domestic abuse. We all have different strategies when it comes to handling negative situations or experiences in our lives. Even though some people have positive strategies, those affected by sexual abuse often turn to negative approaches, such as denial and substance abuse. For people who have been greatly affected, they may show effects, such as anorexia, bulimia, and self–harm. They resort to drug or alcohol misuse because of the societal stigma associated with sexual abuse or rape. Sometimes, abused partners resort to substance misuse as a cheap and convenient solution to drown their sorrows/problems. However, this does not help. Instead, it makes the problems worse as time passes by.

A report published by the Pennsylvania Coalition Against Rape indicated that 79% of rape survivors who took alcohol started drinking for the first time after they were sexually assaulted. The report also indicated that 89% of rape survivors who consumed cocaine started doing it for the first time after they were sexually assaulted. The relationship between sexual violence and substance abuse is evident. Using drugs or turning to strategies such as self-harm can ruin a person's life, which is why the emphasis is on encouraging abused partners to seek support rather than resorting to self-help tactics that exacerbate the problem. Therapeutic intervention is particularly important for people who suffer from PTSD, depression and anxiety. When abuse becomes unbearable and extreme, then the abused partner should take the brave step to end the relationship instead of suffering the extremely negative impact of abuse, which takes a long time to address and lasts a lifetime for some women.

- Emotional Trauma

The fact is that emotional abuse is often recurrent and less pronounced, and in most cases, it takes a significant amount of time for the abused partner to realise that they are being abused. Emotional abuse is more dangerous because when the situation gets worse, the abused partner starts blaming themselves for the abuse they are suffering from. In instances of physical abuse, it is often easy to find evidence, whereas in emotional abuse cases, the signs are always more subtle. When an abuser starts throwing hurtful words at their partner by making snide comments about their physical appearance, telling them they do not deserve love, attention or care, the abused partner begins to believe these nasty remarks and view themselves as such.

At this point, their once-sweet love becomes bitter and begins to hurt badly. Any form of abuse is hurtful and destructive, with its effects lasting both short and long term. In most cases, abused partners remain silent about their experiences because of shame and guilt. They do not want to be judged or condemned by a world full of prejudiced people who like to throw words around without fully understanding someone's story. For this reason, most abused partners stay in abusive relationships and continue to suffer terribly and in silence.

Those who eventually leave their abuser continue to face some level of psychological grief, and this pain may alter their understanding of themselves. This is most common with those who do not have strong family/social support networks. In most cases, the abuser succeeds in isolating their partner because they want them to feel helpless and be highly dependent on them. Emotional abuse, in some cases, leads to a nervous breakdown, and when this happens, the abuser thrives on their malevolent actions. Experts say that "there is no clear clinical definition for this effect of abuse yet, but it loosely translates to a point where the victim experiences emotional and psychological distress which affects her functionality". This happens when the abused partner becomes overwhelmed by the effect of the abuse she has suffered.

The duration of time that the abused person remains in an emotionally and verbally abusive relationship can impact how long-lasting the effects are. The longer they remain, the more likely they are to experience some long-lasting effects on their overall wellbeing. Below are some of the typical effects of abuse:

• Abused partners may begin to question their memory of events. They might find it difficult to remember some of the things that happened to them in the relationship or in other areas of their lives.

• Some abused partners may become either more aggressive or docile than they ordinarily are.

• Some women carry the heavy baggage of guilt and shame with them from the toxic relationship, which limits them in how far and how much they can do to improve their lives.

• Abused people walk on eggshells as they have to be mindful of every word and action so that they will not upset their abusive partner.

• Because of the abused partner's alienation from their social network, they may feel helpless, hopeless and as though they have no shoulder to lean on. Shame also contributes to their hopelessness.

• They also feel used, manipulated, controlled, dejected, useless and unwanted.

Most abused partners feel as though they are responsible for repairing the relationship and put a lot of pressure and stress on themselves in the process. They often end up being overwhelmed by the whole exercise. Some of those who have experienced physical or sexual abuse may get bombarded with a range of emotions, like confusion, anger, fear, or they may feel numb to emotions in the future. Just like with emotional abuse, victims of physical abuse may also have feelings of guilt and shame, even when they have been assaulted. Some women will also try to minimise the effects of abuse by trying to cover their bruises and fabricating lies, even when they require medical attention, in order to cover for their abuser for fear of repercussions or being stigmatised by the wider family/culture/religious folks.

Domestic Abuse/Violence and Reproductive Health

There is enough evidence to support that higher reproductive morbidity is seen among women experiencing domestic violence. Studies conducted in North India have shown an elevated odds ratio of gynaecological symptoms when comparing women with husbands who reported no domestic violence and women who experienced physical and sexual violence. It may be attributed to the fact that abusive men were more likely to engage in extra-marital sex and acquire STDs, thereby placing their wives at risk of acquiring STDs. There was also less condom use reported among such men. These make women more susceptible to HIV infection, and the fear of violent male reactions, both physical and psychological, prevents many women from trying to find out more about it. It also discourages them from getting tested and stops them from getting treatment.

Studies in the northern state of Uttar Pradesh have also shown that unplanned pregnancies are significantly more common among wives of abusive men. Besides this, research has shown that battered women are subject to twice the risk of miscarriage and four times the risk of having a baby that is below average weight. In some places, violence also accounts for a sizeable portion of maternal deaths.

According to an article by the World Health Organization (WHO), first published on April 19th, 2018 and updated in June 2020, "Pregnancy-related deaths and diseases remain unacceptably high. In 2015, an estimated 303 000 women died from pregnancy-related causes, 2.7 million babies died during the first 28 days of life and 2.6 million babies were stillborn. While substantial progress has been made over the past two decades, increased access to, and use of, higher-quality health care during pregnancy and childbirth can prevent many of these deaths and diseases, as well as improve women and adolescent girls' experience of pregnancy and childbirth".

A study conducted on violence against women and its consequences on women's reproductive health and depression was aimed at investigating the current reproductive health (RH) status and depression levels of women, and to clarify the relationships between the violence against women and depression and the RH components. Three hundred women participated in the study. Data was collected from the Women Health Center (WHC) in Prince Faisal Hospital in Rusaifa, Jordan. The findings revealed that around 25.9%, 13.1%, 83.2%, and 65.1% of the women participating had been exposed to physical, sexual and psychological violence, respectively. Around 77.7% of women were using contraceptives, and oral contraceptives and intrauterine devices (IUDs) were the most common family planning methods used. In addition, the results revealed that 50% of women were suffering from significant levels of depression. This shows the relationship between exposure to all forms of violence and reproductive health.

Kristina Fiore stated in her article dated 23 January 2010 that "In some abusive relationships, men may use strategies to force women to become pregnant, including sabotaging their birth control, researchers say. Nearly 20% of women at family clinics across northern California reported that their partner tried to coerce them into having a child, sometimes using methods such as poking holes in condoms or flushing birth control pills down the toilet". Dr Elizabeth Miller of the University of California Davis and colleagues reported online in the journal Contraception: "It was stunning to have this many women seeking reproductive health services saying, 'this has happened to me', lead study author Miller said. She added that the reasons men would want their partners to bear children vary "from things like wanting to leave a legacy, to a straightforward desire for attachment, to having absolute control over her body... There are all of these elements to it".

Dr. Aisha Mays, director of the Teen and Young Adult Clinic at San Francisco General Hospital, said pregnancy coercion is a growing problem that has been around for "quite some time" but is just now being recognised as a major health issue. "It's about power and control," said Mays, who was not involved in the study. "It's another way of saying, 'This girl's taken; this girl's mine.'" Mays said she has seen cases in which a young mother who has a child by another partner has been forced by her new boyfriend to have another baby with him. It is also a way for males to make their partner more dependent on them, according to Amy Bonomi of Ohio State University. "Women in abusive relationships are sometimes forced to bear children as a means to keep them dependent on their partner and sometimes as a means to justify additional— and sometimes more severe—abuse," Bonomi said.

As old as this article is, the issues raised are very much relevant to the current reality across the world. Abusers still use coercion in the form of verbal threats, demands, and physical violence to put pressure on their partner to become pregnant. Religious abusers often insult and criticise their partner, labelling them as "carnal" or "lacking or not exercising their faith" when they do not conceive according to their abuser's timescale. The same applies to those who use women to obtain citizenship in the country in which they reside. They force/manipulate their partner to get pregnant so they can use the child/children to qualify for residency. Abusers go as far as sabotaging birth control by flushing pills down the toilet, breaking condoms, or removing contraceptive rings and patches, etc.

Indeed, previous studies have found an association between partner violence and unintended pregnancy, and new research suggests that a man's attempts to control a woman's reproductive choices may play a role in the association. To investigate, the relationship between domestic abuse and unwanted pregnancies, researchers conducted a survey of women ages 16 to 29 who sought care at family planning clinics in Northern California.

More than half of the women surveyed (53%) reported physical or sexual partner violence. Miller noted that women at family planning clinics tend to have higher rates of abuse than the general population. Among all the women, 19% reported pregnancy coercion and 15% reported birth control sabotage. More than a third of women (35%) who reported either form of what researchers call "reproductive control" also reported partner violence. Altogether, the effect of both partner violence and reproductive control nearly doubled a woman's odds of unintended pregnancy. Sadly, once the woman becomes pregnant, the abuser continues with their abusive behaviour or may enact behaviours to control the outcome of the pregnancy, including violent acts to attempt to induce miscarriage and coercion to either continue or terminate the pregnancy.

When abused women suffer a miscarriage due to one of the reasons above, some abusers will torture her, blaming her for the miscarriage and completely dismissing that their abusive behaviour was the cause of it. This is evident in the cases where the abused partner has already had children without pregnancy complications or miscarriages, but once she is coerced by an abusive man to bear children, the problems start. Some abusers are so selfish that even when their partner goes through the process of miscarriage, they will not even ask how she feels or at least be emotionally supportive during that period. All their focus is on "self" and "sex" for the next pregnancy, despite the emotional and physical state of their hurting partner. The abuser prefers to be completely oblivious to the impact of miscarriages on their partner and are only concerned about their own feelings, desires and demands on her, even though she may be experiencing excruciating pain during the process.

When women who have been abused physically and sexually seek therapy, they are often made to understand that they are not at fault. It is therefore important to seek help to escape the adverse effects of abuse on the abused partner's mental health and other long-term effects that may arise. Women's Aid, domestic abuse services, refuges, etc. recognise the enormous courage it takes for women to escape domestic violence, and they support them and the children involved every step of the way, empowering them to rebuild their lives. For those women who may not have access to the resources above, I would advise them to seek support from trusted family members or friends who will guide them in the right direction.

CHAPTER 7
Breaking the Cycle of Abuse

It is important to understand what the cycle of abuse is before elaborating on this subject, as already mentioned in the previous chapters. According to Jessica DuBois-Maahs's article, dated the 11th of February 2020, "The cycle of abuse is defined by the ways in which an abusive partner keeps a target in a relationship, spanning subtle behaviours as well as physical, visible violence". She further stated that there is a simple tool that describes what occurs in an abusive relationship. It is known as the Power and Control Wheel. It breaks down abusive patterns into four phases, taken from Cynthia Catchings LCSW-S:

• Tension building

• Incident

• Reconciliation

• Calm

Tension Building

"This phase can last anywhere from minutes to weeks. In it, stress builds, and abusers may begin to feel wronged, ignored, or neglected. They may accuse, yell, demand and/or have unrealistic expectations, while the target feels they have to walk on eggshells, are afraid, and become anxious. Targets are likely to be already familiar with the cycle and believe making a small mistake will make the partner angry, so instead they opt to stay quiet or not do something. No matter what is said or done, however, it seems like the target is never right, and a small incident can create a difficult situation in seconds".

The abuser begins to assert their power over their partner in an attempt to control their actions. This is usually done once the abuser has managed to completely isolate their partner from her social networks. Abusers come up with set rules that are hard or impossible to follow, and the partner is told that there will be consequences if they break those rules. Sadly, the consequences usually result in violence against the partner. The rules often include no contact with family members and how money should be spent, including the partner's own salary. Often, every penny will be counted by the controlling, abusive man.

This is more prominent in third-world countries where most families live on a strict budget and women are financially dependent on their husbands/partners or perhaps men earn more than women. The abuser in such cases often creates and monitors a budget for the abused spouse, counting every penny that is spent. This is especially the case if they are responsible for the mortgage or rent for the house, etc. They are sadly oblivious to the cost of seemingly insignificant or minor things, like bills, putting food on the table, personal care products, etc., which come at a high cost for someone who is already struggling financially.

The use of demeaning, degrading and derogatory phrases toward the abused partner usually emerges at this stage, which leads to tension being built up within the couple. However, due to the selfishness and self-centredness of the abuser, they only focus on their own needs and comfort and have no awareness of their partner's needs and feelings.

Unknowingly, the abused partner may internalise their appropriate anger at the abuser's unfairness and experience physical effects, such as depression, tension, anxiety and headaches. As the tension in the relationship increases, minor episodes of violence increase, such as pinching, poking, slapping, shoving, etc. The abused partner works extremely hard to follow the impossible rules set by her abuser in an attempt to prevent the inevitable assaults or emotional abuse. Their efforts get criticised, and no matter how much they try, it is never enough for the abuser, who may not even be able to do half of the tasks that their partner is achieving in a day.

Stress builds up from the pressures of daily life, i.e., conflict over children, childcare responsibilities, marital issues, misunderstandings, or other family pressures/conflicts. It also builds as the result of illness, legal or financial problems, unemployment, or catastrophic events, like floods, rape/sexual abuse or natural disaster. During this period, abusers feel ignored, threatened, annoyed or wronged. The feeling lasts, on average, several minutes to hours, although it may last as long as several months. To prevent more abuse or violence, the abused partner may try to reduce the tension by becoming compliant and nurturing. However, nothing ever pleases abusers. They always find a loophole for abuse and think that their actions are justified.

Incident

This is the stage where violence or acute violence occurs. If the abused partner says or does something the abuser feels upset about or threatened by, the abuser will attempt to dominate their partner through verbal, physical or sexual abuse. Most of the time, the abused partner will keep these incidents a secret and not share what has happened with others. In some serious cases of physical violence, the abused partner ends up in the hospital and even lies to the medical personnel about the cause of their injuries. During this stage, the abuser attempts to dominate their partner from every angle. Outbursts of violence and abuse occur, which may include verbal abuse and psychological abuse.

No wonder many women in abusive relationships suffer with so many illnesses that progress into deadly diseases, which science may never be able to prove. It is easy to focus our attention on physical abuse because it is easy to prove this form of abuse. But questions often arise when the health of a woman who had been happy and healthy prior to getting married or getting into an abusive relationship begins to go drastically downhill, no matter how much she disguises this with a smile on her face day in and day out. This is indicative of ongoing incidents of abuse in her relationship.

In the most extreme cases, where the abuser exhibits uncontrolled and violent outbursts, their actions lead to death. The abuser physically kills/murders his spouse. Whilst this is the shortest of the stages, it is the most dangerous stage of abuse, because in their own mind, the abuser thinks they are teaching their partner a lesson. Sadly, they cause them irreversible hurt or harm that may take a long time to heal if they manage to survive. The injuries may start out as minor things, like marks and bruises, but as the cycle continues, the violence becomes increasingly brutal and escalates into gross bodily harm or death. During the acute stage of violence, if death does not occur—and regardless of whether the abused partner does or does not fight back—they go into a state of physical and psychological shock. The abuser tends to discount these episodes and underestimate their partner's injuries, feel justified for their brutal actions, or turn the story against their partner.

Reconciliation

Following the incident, abusers with a sense of emotions might feel remorse or fear and try to initiate a reconciliation in different forms, i.e., buying flowers, gifts, taking their partner out for dinner or suggesting a nice vacation. They often promise it will be the last time the abuse happens and they, to some extent, acknowledge their wrongdoing, even though they will not take full responsibility for it. At this stage, the abused partner experiences pain, humiliation, disrespect, fear and may be staying for financial reasons or because of the children. The abuser often emphasises that they did not want to do what they did, but the abused partner made them because of their lack of understanding, provocation, disrespect or because they do not listen to the abuser's instructions or advice. In the cycle of violence, the batterer usually begins an intense effort to win forgiveness and ensure that the relationship does not break up. The abuser will ask for forgiveness and behave in a very loving and kind manner for a short period of time.

While abusers apologise, they still blame their victim for the violence, stating things like, "If you had followed my advice or taken my instruction, I would not have reacted that way would not have hit you" or whatever the case may be. Abusers who are financially capable of using gifts to convince their partner to forgive them may do so. However, the majority of abusers are financially dependent on the same women they are abusive and violent towards. The abused partner wants to believe that the abuse will end, and their hopes are supported by abuser's temporarily loving behaviour. It is true that once violence has begun, it continues to increase both in frequency and severity, no matter how deceptive the abuser may be and no matter how many empty promises they make about changing their behaviour.

Change cannot occur unless the abuser seeks support and assistance from trained professionals. Abusers may begin to feel remorse, guilty feelings, or fear that their partner will leave or call the police. The abused partner may feel the pain, fear, humiliation, disrespect, confusion, and may mistakenly feel responsible for standing up against their abuser's ferocious behaviour. Characterised by affection, apology, ignoring the incident, with assurances that the abuser will do their best to change, the abuser often claims that they feel overwhelming remorse and sadness.

Some abusers may use self-harm or threats of suicide to gain sympathy or to prevent their partner from leaving the relationship. This is all done for selfish reasons, so the abuser can continue to use and abuse their partner. Abusers are often very convincing, and some are good talkers who can convince their partner that all is well when it is obviously not. This is why many abused partners who are eager for the relationship to improve for a number of reasons, who are often worn down and confused by longstanding abuse, continue to be entrapped in the abusive relationships with their violent spouse who causes them unimaginable pain and suffering.

Calm

This is also known as the "honeymoon stage", as abusers are kind, calm, interested and may express willingness to engage in counselling, as well as asking for forgiveness. The abused partner wants to believe that the abuser has changed and will accept their apology. However, this does not last long. The abuser will soon start to find little flaws or behaviours that they criticise in a passive-aggressive way and their apologies become less sincere over time. Passive–aggressive behaviour is a way of expressing anger in a seemingly non-hostile way—a deliberate and masked way of expressing covert feelings. It's a behaviour that encompasses more than just eye rolls and faux compliments; it involves a range of actions designed to get back at another person without him or her recognising the underlying anger (Ladan Nikravan Hayes Sep 06, 2018).

Another reason for passive aggression is the person's upbringing. Children who are raised by overly controlling parents, in an environment where self-expression is not permitted, are forced to learn other ways to express feelings of anger and hostility. Since they are dependent upon their parents, they risk punishment if they do not do as their parents say. Therefore, they lash out at their parents covertly and maintain that behaviour into adulthood. Needless to say, most abusers exhibit this behaviour towards their partner at this stage as they do not want to come across as physically aggressive. This is an indication that their unaddressed behaviour is beginning to resurface, despite their promises to change. The cycle then returns to the tension-building phase. The effect of the continual cycle may include a loss of love, increased contempt and distress, physical disability, separation, divorce and, at the extreme, homicide or murder.

Breaking the Cycle of Abuse

While every relationship is different, most abusive relationships have one aspect in common: the abuser takes action to have more power and control over their partner. This makes it difficult for some people to realise that they are in an abusive relationship, as their abuser may disguise his behaviour or character in the early stages of the relationship. Often, controlling and possessive behaviours do not rear their ugly heads until the bonds of a relationship grow tight. It is therefore important to understand the Power and Control Wheel and how the cycle of abuse works, as this can help a person determine if they are caught in an abusive relationship or not. Additionally, learning about community resources and seeking guidance and assistance from professionals can also make it easier to leave a relationship when an abused person is ready to do so.

The best way to end the cycle of abuse is through psychoeducation and the help of a mental health professional. Catchings said, "It takes an individual up to 12 times to leave for good. It is also known that the first times a target leaves, is mostly to test the waters and see if they can survive. Learning about what it is like to escape and plan to survive alone is what might create the constant in-and-out in an abusive relationship as well".

Therapy provides abused partners with a place to vent, receive support, heal and forgive, all of which are necessary aspects of ending the cycle of abuse. It can also help educate the abused person about the patterns of abusive behaviour, as well as explore possible early trauma that may contribute to their unhealthy relationship expectations. If an abused partner believes something is not right in their relationship and cannot confront the situation on their own, therapy can help. While the abuser's control may prevent her from seeking in-person care, online therapy can be a great option for privacy and safety. For immediate support, abused partners should contact the National Domestic Violence Hotline for the country in which they live.

Breaking the cycle of abuse is extremely difficult and may at times seem impossible. The very nature of abuse is wrapped up in power and dominance. To break the cycle is to break out of the powerful control the abuser has over their partner. But victims always have to remember that they are worth more than their abusers would have them believe and they do have the power to break out of an abusive relationship, no matter how tough and gloomy things may seem. The vicious cycle of domestic abuse can become harder and harder to break the longer the person tolerates it and waits to disrupt the pattern.

According to Dr McGee, the first step in breaking out is often gaining an awareness that what is going on is, in fact, domestic abuse. "For many victims, this realization comes after talking to someone about what has been happening at home. Sometimes when people are able to talk about it with someone who is not going to judge them or demand they take an action immediately, they are finally able to see just how serious the situation is," he says. "For the first time, they can actually hear themselves". This is crucial as people are very quick to judge others without having a full understanding of what is going on in the other person's life. Therefore, caution has to be taken, especially when confiding in some religious figures or family members, who may be biased about the situation by virtue of their association or relationship with the abuser.

As hard as it may be, the path to healing could begin with a few simple steps: telling someone trustworthy, seeking counselling, talking to a friend, Women's Aid or shelter worker or the designated domestic abuse workers in their local area. It may be incredibly hard to find the words to tell someone about the abuse or to even know where to start, but speaking those difficult words is the only way to make a positive change.

An article by Sam Houston from State University, published April 7th, 2016, stated that "Victims of domestic violence are hindered from leaving their abusers by internal and external factors, including the response of the criminal justice system, fear, perceived control, and self-esteem, according to the latest report from the Crime Victims' Institute. The report, 'Breaking the Cycle of Intimate Partner Violence,' is designed to provide criminal justice professionals with information about the factors that influence a victim's willingness to leave an abusive relationship or to prosecute their abuser".

"Domestic violence has historically been viewed as a family matter that should be settled within the home," said Leana Bouffard of State University, co-author of the study with graduate student Amanda Goodson.

Houston continued to state that "The biggest external factors that influence the victim's decision to leave are the criminal justice system, including the lengthy process, police attitudes and procedures, the removal of the offender, and the lack of social support. Internal factors that weigh on victims include increased levels of fear; negative emotions such as guilt, shame, helplessness, and embarrassment; or mental health issues such as post-traumatic stress disorder and depression".

I have come across a number of people who, despite suffering extreme abuse at the hands of their partner, are petrified of pursuing or supporting police prosecution because they are unable to prove their experience, particularly when there has been no physical assault.

As a result of their fear and anxiety, the abused partner often does not want to appear in court and be further humiliated by their abuser, who, as mentioned earlier in the book, has captured false evidence earlier on to use against her, portraying her as the perpetrator and denying their abusive actions. It appears that many domestic violence courts have adopted key elements, such as interagency collaboration, working closely with independent domestic abuse agencies, social services, housing department, police, etc. in order to improve their decision-making and enhance safety planning aimed at reducing domestic violence.

Breaking the cycle of abuse amongst abusers is something that strongly relies upon honesty, humility, courage, strength, and a strong will. If these are lacking in the abuser's personal life, they will find it difficult to break this cycle. Abusers need to be honest and humble enough with themselves to accept that their behaviour is unacceptable and is causing harm to their partner and any children who may be trapped in this unhealthy atmosphere. As much as the abused partner needs to seek support to deal with the trauma and hurt, they have been subjected to, the same applies to the abuser. Without support, they will simply carry on with this atrocity, moving from one woman to the next.

For abusers to get started on the right path, they need to seek support from those who can help. This makes things a bit easier and makes navigating the process much smoother. Support can come in different forms: therapy, professional counselling, advice from family members or friends, or religious leaders, spiritual support, etc.

•   Therapy: Abusers might need to undergo therapy if they have passed the stage where they can benefit from support from their local community. This may be difficult to admit at first, but when they finally confess to domestic abuse professionals, they can then be referred to the relevant professionals or specialists. These professionals may conduct assessments in order to put appropriate support in place. This requires open-mindedness and willingness to build a positive working relationship with the professionals or therapist involved in the process. Abusers have to bear in mind that the success of any therapy depends on the therapist and client finding some common ground. A shared understanding will help them achieve their goal and allow them to rediscover themselves along this journey as they face some unpleasant truths.

•   Professional counselling: This is not exactly therapy, but it is quite close. Some professional counsellors deal with domestic violence and abusive patterns to help abusers break free from the cycle of violence they are trapped in. These days, some men are becoming more aware of the importance of addressing the issue of their abusive behaviour and are seeking professional support.

•   Advice from friends, family members, etc.: Another option that abusers can explore is seeking advice from friends, family members, or spiritual leaders. Undoubtedly, among their friends or family members, there is someone who is held in high regard and who the abuser can confide in at difficult times. Seek intelligence and wisdom from those who show true love and endurance in their relationships, asking for tips on how to build a peaceful home. As this is a delicate issue, abusers cannot talk to just anybody. The people they choose should have a sense of maturity in order to offer practical, positive advice that the abuser can follow.

• Apologise to their partner for the hurt they have caused: As difficult as this can be, it is vital for the abuser to swallow their pride and try to talk things over with their partner. They must find ways to communicate with their partner, where appropriate, and begin by offering a sincere apology. They should demonstrate a genuine desire to become better, followed by actions towards this goal. Some abusers often pay what is called "lip service", meaning they never mean what they say. Instead, they often lay out a number of rules and regulations that have to be followed by their partner in order to avoid the subsequent incidents of abuse. Abusers have to remember that they are seeking to overcome a problem at this stage and have to forget about laying out orders as usual. The worst thing they can do at this stage is to justify their actions and give justifications like "you pushed me" or "you caused me to hit you". Nothing could be worse than this. The majority of the time, the abused partner is not willing to talk to their abuser at this stage, and this is totally fine and understandable. They may still be hurting or injured, and they are likely also be trying to come to terms with the impact of the abuse. If they choose not to talk to their abuser, then this should be respected, and no force or manipulation should be used to convince them to communicate when they are not ready.

Westmarland, N. and Kelly, L. and Chalder-Mills, J. (2010) "Domestic violence perpetrator programmes: what counts as success?", London Metropolitan University and Durham University, London and Durham, dated the 7th of January 2014, shows the research undertaken as part of a pilot study designed to feed into a larger programme of research on domestic violence perpetrator programmes. The research participants were self-selecting and came from five UK domestic violence perpetrator programmes, where the views of four groups were sought:

- 22 men who were in or had completed perpetrator programmes.

- 18 female partners/ex-partners of men in perpetrator programmes (not all of whom were linked to the men interviewed).

- 6 funders/commissioners of perpetrator programmes.

- 27 programme practitioners (including perpetrator group work facilitators, women's support workers and managers).

However, I would like us to look at the views of the abused partners/ex-partners and the perpetrators. A total of 73 interviews were undertaken, and all of the participants were involved with organisations that were signed up to the Respect Service Standard, which means that they provided an integrated support service to the partners and ex-partners of men who attended the perpetrator programmes. The programmes worked with men mandated to attend by family courts and child protection services, as well as those who self-referred and were asked to attend by their partners. It seems that this programme was beneficial for both groups those who remained in the relationship and for those who did not. Where there are children involved, the abused partners and the perpetrators are always in each other's lives for contact when perpetrators committed to it. It is therefore helpful for perpetrators to participate in programmes like this to avoid the continuation of conflict during contact handover times when they have already separated and no longer live together.

What success meant to abused partners/ex-partners

Six themes emerged. Starting with the most frequently mentioned, they were:

- respectful/improved relationships

- expanded space for action

- support/decreased isolation

- enhanced parenting

- reduction or cessation of violence and abuse

- man understanding the impact of domestic violence

The first thing to note here is that ending violence comes relatively low down (fifth) in this list, with the most noted and valued outcome being establishing a respectful/ improved relationship. Whilst this might require, by definition, violence and abuse to be absent, this was implicit in women's responses.

It is reported that "For those who stayed with the men the changes which were referred to included doing more as a family, feeling happier, having a better, stronger partnership and staying together as a couple. The words used to describe what was different about the men included them being more thoughtful, supportive, respectful, calm, or alternatively less moody. Open and respectful communication was at the core of these shifts, for example, being able to talk about difficult issues, negotiate, express opinions, open up and talk about feelings. Many women spoke of having a new sense that their partner was willing not just to listen but also to hear and understand their point of view, and that of their children. Everyday acts, such as making a cup of tea in the following example, symbolised deeper realignments in relationships that were associated with increased respect. Being able to enter the house without being scared, stay out late without feeling she would have to "walk on eggshells" the next day, spend time with family and friends are all examples of what we term expanded space for action".

What success meant to men on perpetrator programmes

Three core themes emerged:

Starting with the most frequent, they were:

- enhanced awareness of self and others

- reduction or cessation of violence and abuse

- improved relationship with better communication

Research shows that "Enhanced awareness of self and others covers the ability to monitor and understand self and others' feelings and emotions and use this knowledge to guide thinking and action. The men talked about a range of examples that fitted under this heading, including emotional self-awareness, self-control, empathy and responsiveness to others. They described themselves as being more patient, having a greater ability to control and moderate their own behaviour, having different reactions to situations and generally being able to engage better with everyone.

The ability to self-reflect, clearly something that is required in programmes, and improved communication skills were important and valued gains for some men. This chimed with women's responses, especially when men talked about their newfound ability to listen and understand her point of view. Understanding the impact of domestic violence on others was an important part of this. The reduction or cessation of violence and abuse was discussed more often and more explicitly than in the interviews with women, undoubtedly in part because programme content focuses on this. Many men maintained they had already made this change".

Having an improved relationship with better communication also emerged as a strong theme for men during the research. Being honest within a relationship was mentioned regularly, as was being able to rebuild and sustain it. The men recognised that going back to previous patterns was not an option if the frequently mentioned goal of not losing their partner was to be an outcome of the programme and their change of behaviour. One man, for example, explained that he had previously attended a number of anger management courses, but that these had simply taught him to remove himself from the situation rather than to be able to openly and honestly communicate his feelings: He stated "... I've just found that, you know, if you communicate with people from an open, honest place, you're generally going to get that back. If you, you know, if you're communicating with someone with fire, with aggression—they're going to be defensive...".

For abusers or perpetrators who are truly determined to become better men who no longer resort to abuse to feel good, then they have to make that resolution and be determined to stick to it. They need to set their heart on it and feed their minds with positive information that will assist them in their journey towards living a peaceful life. Of course, there will be some difficult and testing times, but this is part of the journey that one has to face when striving for a better life, and it helps to measure the progress made. This is all done with one aim and for one purpose: to break the cycle of abuse and violence before causing irreversible damage to those on the receiving end.

CHAPTER 8
The importance of self-love and self-respect to end abuse inclinations

Maxwell Maltz said, "low self-esteem is like driving through life with your handbrake on", and this is as true as life itself. There is no way that an abuser can enjoy life and love their family if they do not love and value themselves. And if an abuser cannot love himself, there is no way he can genuinely love his partner. Self-love, self-care, self-respect, and self-value are essential to the success of any relationship.

Self-love

It is effortless for people to say they love themselves. But this can only be seen in their actions. Love is not just an emotional affair; it is really a matter of words and actions. Self-love is not selfish; instead, it is an appreciation of oneself and a conscious effort to achieve the best you can for yourself. Love harbours no form of hatred, violence or ill-wish. When people love themselves as they ought, they acknowledge that despite their shortcomings and not always getting things right, they fully understand their worth and always strive to be better, happy and content with themselves.

If a man loves himself as a husband or partner and a father, then the people who matter most to him will enjoy the same love. Breaking free from the cycle of domestic violence and other forms of domestic abuse requires abusers to rekindle the love they once had for themselves before they became abusive and violent. Below are some important things abusers can do to love themselves better:

•   They can verbally express love to themselves

A Meaningful Life Centre article titled "How to love yourself unconditionally" states "Self-love is inherent in every one of us, and necessary for living a wholesome life. But then why do so many people dislike themselves? On the other hand: Is there a form of unhealthy self-love that breeds selfishness and arrogance? And how is that different from healthy self-love that fosters self-esteem and self-confidence? How does one create a positive balance between self-love, humility, and selflessness? Can you love another if you do not love yourself? With so much left wanting in the healthy, loving role models in our lives—it should not come as a surprise the confusion we have about these matters".

Practicing self-love can be challenging for many people, especially those who never experienced love from their parents or primary carers earlier in life. Love is not about being self-absorbed or narcissistic; it is about getting in touch with oneself in order to live joyfully and happily, not only with oneself but with others, too. It is important for abusers to learn to love themselves unconditionally in a healthy manner that helps them reclaim their personal dignity and self-respect.

An article-Lifehack by Jessie Hayes on self-love stated "do yourself a favour, take a deep breath, give yourself a little hug and start practicing the following: Start each day by telling yourself something really positive. How well you handled a situation, how lovely you look today. Anything that will make you smile. Surround yourself with people who love and encourage you. Let them remind you just how amazing you are".

I am aware that this may be extremely difficult to do for men who have never experienced love and warmth, especially from the male figures in their lives. However, taking one step at a time to transform their lives and their perception of themselves will eventually lead to positive results.

This requires abusers to step outside their comfort zone and try something new that will allow them to experience this incredible feeling. They will come to realise they have achieved something they did not know they could. Patience and persistence are also required to practice self-love daily and consistently. Once they have mastered self-love, abusers will begin to treat others with love and respect and will feel better about themselves. However, this does not necessarily mean it will be reciprocated by others, but this should not be disheartening.

Family members should be a vital part of this process, if the family relationships have not broken down completely. Reaching out to family members, friends and close associates who will support them and hold their hand through this journey and the hurdles it may present are important. Abusers cannot change the past, but they can control their future by focusing on believing in their ability to change and forgiving themselves for the wrongdoing and the torture they inflicted on those who loved them dearly. Of course, they may feel embarrassed and ashamed of their actions, but they should try to let go of that shame. This goes back to the subject of apologising to their partner genuinely.

- Always be honest and realistic with themselves

Men who live in denial do not value themselves. It is good to always tell the truth, even in the midst of turmoil and conflict. Some abusive men are incorrigible liars who believe their own lies—hence being sceptical and suspicious about everything concerning their partner. These are the same abusers who often accuse their partner of lying and are brave enough to say, "I don't believe you". Why is this so? It is because of their own lies and the untruthful lives they lead? They, in turn, believe that everyone lives according to their lying habits and sadly torture innocent souls as a result of this attitude. Abusers are good at fabricating lies and can accuse their partners of the craziest things one could ever think of.

Due to how the minds of abusers function, they can come up with fabricated reasons to justify their accusations against their partner. For example, after a certain woman got married to an abuser for some time who had caused her high levels of anxiety, she struggled to sleep as a result of the trauma and threats to kill that had been made by the abuser. So, she started hyperventilating, having hot flushes, and experiencing reflex actions in the initial stages of her sleep, etc. The abuser who had previously expressed his understanding of these symptoms started accusing her of masturbating on their matrimonial bed in his presence.

This had never been the case until the woman, who was extremely unwell at the time, had refused to have sex due to the state of her physical health. Despite all the explanations given by the woman about the levels of anxiety she was going through, the abuser insisted this was not anxiety but "masturbation addiction" and claimed he had done the research on it. However, when asked by his wife to do research on the symptoms of anxiety, similar to what she was exhibiting physically, the abuser became paranoid and more abusive and violent. He wanted his wife to admit that he was "right, as always", causing more psychological trauma to his wife and cursing her to die for "lying". This is a typical example of how abusers cause so much emotional and psychological damage due to their paranoia and self-deceit.

I like the proverb "Honesty is the best policy" because telling the truth, no matter how hard it may be for some people, liberates one's soul and allows them to experience indescribable peace. However, it appears that most abusers live a life of lies and dishonesty. This is really sad because all they do is spend their life covering their own back whilst pointing the finger at innocent people. They may have had some experiences where they were lied to, but this does not mean they should be making false accusations and making their innocent partner pay for the sins of others. Once the abuser accepts their own flaws and inadequacies, they will find it easy to understand and accept the truth from their partner. Most importantly, accepting that there are things they can never be proud of on their life journey leads to the right path—the path of honesty—instead of playing the blame game and not being truthful and honest with themselves.

- Let go of the traumatic experiences and wounds

In *Healing from Childhood Trauma*, E.B. Johnson, (NLP-MP, Apr 15, 2019) stated "It's not impossible. It's just hard. Childhood trauma is caused by any situation in which a child perceives that they are in an extremely frightening, dangerous or overwhelming position. Traumatic events cause children to feel helpless and scared in a way that is far beyond their mental and emotional processing. These situations can occur in one-off events like natural disasters and injuries—or they could occur from regular instances of physical, sexual and verbal abuse. All these events can bring on symptoms of emotional and psychological trauma, and all of these events can haunt children well into their adult lives".

The majority of abusive men across the world have suffered from traumatic childhood experiences, but sadly, most of them are in complete denial of these events. Over the years, I have observed that abusers from certain parts of the world do not accept that they were brought up in abusive communities and family environments. Whilst they may tell stories about their traumatic and very harsh upbringing, they refuse to acknowledge that their upbringing was abusive. I am not talking about those who claim to have been abused just because they had strict rules and boundaries and perhaps were physically chastised, depending on where they live in the world, I am talking about childhood abuse in its different forms.

When a person experiences childhood trauma, their life is changed significantly, and it seems that most people in the world have experienced childhood trauma one way or the other. However, depending on how these experiences have been dealt with or addressed, the majority of people are able to overcome it and not let these experiences shape their future relationships with others. With regards to abusers, traumatic experiences often remain unaddressed and suppressed, thereby changing their character and destroying their ability to foster caring and nurturing relationships, even decades after the traumatic events. When left unaddressed, childhood trauma holds the abuser's life back and bricks up their potential in unimaginable ways. Regrettably, abusers' hearts are damaged, and their perception of life is altered as they build high, impenetrable walls around themselves, thus making it harder to find the psychological and emotional healing they unknowingly require.

One of the effects of trauma is passive-aggressive behaviour, which is quite common amongst abusers. Adult survivors of childhood trauma usually carry a lot of anger that they do not know how to deal with. As stated above, rather than confronting and dealing with these painful emotions head-on, they choose to bury them, resorting to passive-aggressive behaviour that can isolate them and destroy important relationships in their lives. Apart from the violent behaviour some may display, other abusers often strike out with cynicism they call "jokes" or "mistakes" that they claim were innocent. They do not feel comfortable showing their anger because they do not know what will happen if they do. Instead, they act out passive-aggressively, protecting their already troubled soul in a self-defeating manner.

Healing the harm and hurt of one's childhood is one the hardest things to do, but it is necessary for everyone who is hurting to create the life they want. For abusers to get over the past, they have to start by facing it and bravely taking one step at a time. This is why it is important for them to be honest with themselves about their emotional state to understand why they feel the way they do. Trauma can trigger momentous emotions, and unless they learn how to process these emotions, abusers will continue to repeat the same damaging patterns that keep them trapped in a cycle of hurting their partner and children. Refusing to face the problem and seek support to address childhood trauma causes issues to fester like sores and release negative energy that damages their intimate relationships and their family, social, employment and business relationships.

Research further shows that childhood trauma is associated with various forms of emotional dysregulation, as well as stress-reactivity, which is believed to be one of the links between childhood trauma and physiological disorders. "Those who experienced emotionally abusive environments growing up are more likely to show stronger reactivity to stress and more interpersonal problems as adults. These effects manifest themselves in strange ways throughout our adult lives no matter how much time and space may separate us from the event". Learning how to recognise these manifestations of childhood issues without denying their existence is the core of healing, but I am mindful that these can also be uncomfortable to face.

Healing a trauma starts with understanding it and the vast array of emotions that can come along with it. Hence the importance of understanding trauma and how it affects one personally. This can be a really difficult challenge, and it requires the abuser to turn to others for support. Once they have a trusted person to talk to and let go of the past, abusers begin to feel like a weight has been lifted off their shoulders. They start to see the light at the end of the tunnel. Finding a place where they will feel comfortable, calm, positive and peaceful is of utmost importance and should be at the top of their priority list during the healing process.

Having the support of a mental health professional throughout the process ensures that the abuser is able to address traumatic triggers in a safe space. It is important to choose a validating, trauma-informed counsellor who can meet their needs and who is able to guide them through the appropriate therapeutic steps to address symptoms and triggers. Some people benefit from EMDR therapy (eye movement desensitisation and reprocessing therapy), which enables them to process their trauma without being re-traumatised in the process.

However, experts state that "the therapy that works for one person may not necessarily work for another depending on their specific symptoms, the severity of the trauma and the length of time a person has been traumatized". Throughout this journey of healing from trauma, abusers need to learn to be compassionate towards themselves whilst facing the darkness of their past. It is normal to suffer from noxious shame and self-blame for being abusive and violent towards others. That said, it is crucial that they are gentle towards themselves during this journey and acknowledge the difficulties involved in healing and transformation.

Self-respect and self-value

Self-respect is a product of self-love, and when abusers begin to love themselves better, they learn to respect themselves. Self-respect is the respect they have for themselves, as opposed to ego, which is the understanding of their own importance. I understand that an inflated ego may be generated from having a lot of self-esteem or when people view themselves as too important and special. This is the typical behaviour exhibited by some abusers with huge egos. They feel superior to others and want to dominate and control them whilst deep inside they feel worthless and undeserving of respect. For those who respect themselves, the ego is still naturally present, but it does not play a huge part in their actions and maintain self-respect and self-control.

Self-respect is not just about having a high sense of personal worth. It is also about knowing how to behave and present oneself in a way that fosters respect from other people. If abusers are determined to love and respect themselves, then certain aspects of their life will have to change, and their idea of self-respect should not be based on violence and nasty behaviour towards their partner. Self-respect should never be mistaken for pride or arrogance. It is truly remarkable to see the change in abusers when they begin to see their worth and understand that self-respect is a necessity for the success of their relationship. As people begin to see how well the abuser conducts themselves and how well they exercise self-restraint and control, it is only natural that they automatically relax and respond positively in a reciprocal manner.

While it is important to respect their partner in a relationship, the abuser is never able to achieve this if they have no self-respect. Self-respect and acceptance of oneself is the key to building confidence and maintaining healthy relationships with other people. Showing respect to themselves means that the abuser is recognising their worth and value in the process of rediscovery, and this can be done in different ways. For example, finding a hobby, engaging in community projects, learning new skills, etc. It may be that the abuser's self-value has been crushed and bruised by their abusive behaviour towards their partner over the years, and they may be dented by their guilt of being a perpetrator of domestic violence. Nevertheless, recognising and feeling guilty about their own actions should not be a hindrance to their zeal to change. Rather, it should be a driving force behind their recovery.

The impact of self-love and self-value on an abuser's family

As mentioned earlier, it is natural for a partner to respond lovingly when they see their spouse make an effort to transform their behaviour. For unbroken relationships, this attempt is usually appreciated by the partner, who plays a significant role in the process of the abuser's reformation. It is through the desire to rebuild the relationship and taking steps to work towards this that the family of the abuser can begin to breathe again and support them on the road to recovery. Of course, this will not happen immediately—it usually happens gradually, over time. As the abuser embraces these positive efforts and gestures in their life, they will begin to love, value, and appreciate their family more.

The Domestic Violence Prevention Centre Gold Coast Inc. recognises that men who try to become better have a better chance of breaking the domestic violence cycle and can go on to improve their relationship with their partner. Domestic violence is not always something done by accident. It is often a planned and strategic move to keep the abused partner subdued and controlled. It is a grand plan to make partner agree with their abuser or withhold their own opinion. Reversing this situation should be one of the main goals of therapy. Thus, as the abuser begins to show their partner love and respect, stemming from their newly discovered self-love and self-respect, they will be showing their partner that they are ready to respect and accept their wishes and opinions. Embracing love and respect will eventually impact positively on the abuser's family, and as their sense of self-worth increases, so will their sense of responsibility.

An article from 2020 on "Reducing the Risk of Domestic Abuse", taken from The Guardian UK Edition on the 23rd of May 2016, reported a poignant urge by a reformed domestic abuser/perpetrator named Vic Tamati in New Zealand, who was brave enough to call on men to break the cycle of violence at a rally in Auckland, protesting the death of a three-year-old. Vic who abused his family for decades made a galvanising call for the country to become a domestic violence-free zone. The article stated "In a powerful speech in Auckland on Sunday, Vic Tamati, an anti-domestic violence campaigner, admitted to beating his own family members for thirty-eight years. Tamati said he knew no better, as he was beaten with a machete as a child by his own father".

He continued "The last one I bashed up was my eight-year-old daughter because she didn't go to school," Tamati told a 1,000-strong crowd. "All I thought was, 'as long as I don't bash them the way my dad bashed me'. My dad bashed me with a machete. And I chose not to bash my kids with a machete, but I did everything else. I didn't know any better. I thought I was OK". Tamati was speaking at a rally calling for an end to child abuse in New Zealand, following the death of three-year-old Moko Rangitoheriri at the hands of his carers the previous year. "I want to ask all the men here today to take up the challenge and the challenge is this: that we, as men, declare Aoteroa New Zealand a family violence-free zone," said Tamati. "I grew up in the darkness. I thought that bashing up was OK, as long as I didn't hit them with a machete. I was so, so wrong. I did nearly 40 years of violence. I am responsible for the death of two people, ruled as accidents by the coroners' court. Those two people aren't coming back. And nor is Moko".

What an emotional and yet inspirational example of a once-abusive man who is responsible for killing or murdering two people, coming out in public to challenge other men to stop the abuse. I believe that Vic must have gone through a long process of reformation after acknowledging his abusive behaviour and desiring a change. His story is proof that any abuser can change as long as they put their heart into it. He stated that he grew up in darkness and knew no better. I have no doubt that his father's upbringing was the same and he also knew no better. Nevertheless, Vic chose to change the course of his life when he got the knowledge he needed. You may be reading this book today and wondering how to proceed from here. My advice is that you follow the simple steps and tips given previously and remember that "Rome was not built in a day". Determination and persistence will lead you to the right destination: reformation or modification of your behaviour.

An article by Heidi Davoren, posted on Sunday the 10th of May 2015, updated on the 27th of September 2015, on domestic violence, reported a story of a reformed perpetrator named Jerry Retford who called on abusers to "take responsibility". Jerry Retford used to abuse his wife—physically, verbally and emotionally. His violence was also witnessed by his two children. It appears that Mr Retford turned his life around after attending a Relationships Australia programme that helps violent men acknowledge and change their abusive behaviours. He wanted to share his story in the hopes that it would encourage other men to seek help, and also because he wanted to take responsibility for his actions.

Mr Retford stated, "I'm very proud of who I am today and the changes that I've made that have made me the man I am today". He added, "I guess I want to share in the hope that it will help, not only other men, but other relationships and help people who have been in the same position". His turning point came when he realised the impact his abusive behaviour was having on his children, who were witnesses to it and obviously living in a very unhealthy environment characterised by violence and strife. Although it took a divorce and another relationship before Mr Retford actually sought help.

He stated, "Whilst I wasn't physically abusive in the relationships after my divorce, I was verbally and emotionally abusive. And, thankfully, that person had the skills to say 'that's not OK in this relationship. Go and get some help".

Ignoring his partner and being in denial could have been an easy option for him, but despite the end of that relationship, he sought the support/help that he needed, stating, "I am grateful to her for the catalyst that brought about so much change in me and also so grateful to the wonderful people at Relationships Australia for the Taking Responsibility course and the amazing men that I did that course with, who actually showed me no matter what else is going on in a relationship, the only thing I can fix is me. And I need to take responsibility for that if I want to get well. Instead of blaming everyone else for what was going on, I started looking at me and how I can change me, and it was a phenomenal process".

This shows that once an abuser decides to do away with self-pride and selfishness and focus on what is right, they can access support to change their life. All it takes is a decision and eagerness to make changes. It is similar to the way they choose to act abusively and aggressively. Domestic abuse can be vanquished by those who are willing to do what it takes, no matter how tough and long the journey may be. As a learned behaviour, they can unlearn it through help and replace it with positive and useful habits that would greatly help repair their relationship with their partner and their loved ones at large.

Mr Retford also stated, "In terms of my life, my healed life, compared to my unhealed life, I guess I've been going well for five or six years now, out of 45 years. It's easy to say, 'I just lose control when that happens', but we actually make a choice to use violence. Albeit a totally misguided and unconscious choice—it is still a choice". He added, "It is an endorphin addiction, an adrenalin addiction, a rage addiction, which is such a big thing in society today, for example, road rage. The level of rage in people today and their inability to manage what is going on is a contributing factor".

Retford continued, "I still react to things. I do not feel anger anymore, I do not make my partner responsible for my feelings. I do not blame her for what is going on in my life. Life with my partner now is so peaceful. We have not had an angry word in the five or so years we've been together, and we both understand that our own stuff is our own stuff and you don't need to dump that on the other person. We take responsibility". How inspirational is this, knowing the journey these two men went through and how they endured the process for the positive outcomes that they reaped at the end of the programmes. Support for abusers or perpetrators of violence is available in every country, but this requires abusers to step up and eagerly seek this kind of help, not only for their own benefit but for the benefit of their family members.

CHAPTER 9
From abusers to role models

Several societies and groups that advocate for the end of domestic abuse agree that men can take an active part in the fight against domestic violence. Abusive men can be a part of this crusade in several intentional ways while they seek to change their approach and find better strategies to deal with their emotions. It is imperative to keep in mind that they are also making a conscious effort to help put an end to domestic abuse and violence in its different forms. In the previous chapters, we talked about domestic violence, how to address it, and we also talked about how men who are determined to change their lives can go through therapy or counselling to achieve their goals. In this chapter, we will focus on how men can be role models to their children and also help them stop being violent and abusive.

We know how important the role of the father is in our society; raising, nurturing and training children is a responsibility that should be shared between parents. Unfortunately, there are many broken families where children are raised by single parents. Various studies on juvenile education have shown that children and young adults are influenced by the people they spend the most time with. This influence can be positive or negative. If a child spends most of their time at home around a toxic parental relationship, they unconsciously learn this behaviour and are likely to model it as they develop. It goes without saying that no matter how good an abuser is with their children's practical and day-to-day activities and interactions, they do not set a good example when they are abusive to their children's mother or any female figures in their lives.

In discussing this further, we will look at the vital issues concerning family and also the way men ought to treat and relate to their children. I understand that in some societies, men have a vital role in the upbringing and the shaping of children's characters, especially boys. This may be difficult for an abuser to achieve until they have taken steps to transform their life and reconnected with their family. Abusers have to go through the stages of reconciliation and healing before their children (depending on their ages) and family members can learn to trust them again. Once this has been achieved, it is then that reformed abusers can begin to play a significant role in the lives of their family members and be considered trustworthy and responsible. This is a very delicate process that should be handled with the utmost attention and care.

Abusers with their families and children

On the 4th of December 2019, West Yorkshire Police in the United Kingdom launched a new campaign aimed at perpetrators of domestic abuse. They stated, "We do a lot of work to encourage those affected by domestic abuse to break the cycle and seek help. Our message with this campaign is that, ultimately, it is in the perpetrators' hands and their hands only to change their behaviour for good". This is absolutely true, as nothing changes in people's lives unless there is a fire burning in their souls to make the changes they desire. Yorkshire Police stated, "There are organisations across West Yorkshire, who are completely independent of the police, who help both men and women to address the root causes of their violent or controlling behaviour and change their mindset.

While they do work with people who have been arrested, it does not need to get to that stage, and we are encouraging people to make the call now before it gets that far".

Whilst this campaign was launched in Yorkshire, it reflects many other campaigns launched worldwide. In the previous chapter, we saw examples of men who reached out for support, endured the process and came out victorious. Their families were part of the process, and this seems to have worked for them as they were able to repair their relationships. This is not the case for every family that is traumatised by abuse, but support is beneficial for families whose relationships have not completely broken down irreparably. However, this should not stop an abuser from seeking support, as the problem lies with them personally, not their intimate partner.

Yorkshire Police further stated, "Families can be torn apart by domestic abuse, but we also know a lot of people want to do what they can to keep their family together. Ultimately, the earlier that you get help to understand and change the way you behave, the better chance you have of fixing your relationship with your partner and protecting any children in your household".

Children are wonderful, and from young ages, they begin to pick up words and actions from their primary caregivers and the members of their household. This goes on to form their core values later in life. For this reason, every adult should make it their duty and responsibility to behave in an acceptable and appropriate manner around children. The manner in which adults, especially parents, interact with children in their early lives has a huge impact on their general wellbeing later in life. The bond or connection between a child and their parents is sacred, and if anything threatens it, the results are never pleasant.

Becoming a role-model for their children

I believe there are difficulties in adjusting and adapting to a normal life after undergoing behavioural modification following a period of being abusive, no matter how long or short that has been. The behavioural change process is a gradual journey, one that takes the person on a path to soundness and inner peace. It is therefore important to focus on the following in this process:

- Spending time with their children or stepchildren

Fathers who make the choice to devote their time to engaging with their children seem to develop strong relationships with them that cannot be broken. This time spent reflects how they value and love them, despite the competing demands of life, i.e., work. Some men in different societies take the primary role of caregiver for their children, depending on their family structure and arrangement with their partner, who may be the breadwinner or who perhaps earn more than them. Whatever the case may be, these fathers develop a positive relationship with their children, form strong emotional bonds, provide them with safety, security, comfort and model how healthy relationships should work.

It appears that decades of research have focused on mother–child attachment security, but there is much less research on the father–child relationship and how a secure attachment relationship is formed. Nevertheless, in circumstances where fathers are not only present but are available to contribute to the upbringing of their children, therefore spending quality time with them, a positive environment for interaction and the sharing of ideas is created. Fathers in this category are never abusive and never hurt their children or partner due to the strong emotional bond or connection they develop with their family. This simple act helps the children to learn about communing and bonding with one another, and this becomes part of their normal life.

For abusive men, the opposite happens. Instead of focusing on developing and building positive relationships with their partner and children, they aim to destroy the relationships between the mother and her children. Because of their selfishness and self-centeredness, the abuser wants to be put first in everything, forgetting that their abusive behaviour interferes with this. Once they feel they are not prioritised by their partner due to their abusive behaviour, they despise any positive relationship between their spouse and their children. Regrettably, some go as far as neglecting their own children's needs, as they spitefully refuse to engage in their daily activities. What they do not realise is that they will never form solid relationships with their children, except through emotional manipulation and mind games, as the children develop.

Children are sensitive and pick up on those negative emotions from their father. They eventually become avoidant, not wanting to engage in any activities with their abusive father. The majority of the time, abusers do not even take the time to learn anything about their children's activities and hobbies. Oddly, the abusers who do not take part in their children's welfare and day-to-day activities are the ones who are not financially responsible and are dependent on their partner for their own needs to be met.

During the process of behavioural modification, it is not easy for men to engage in their children's activities because they do not know how to relate to them or participate. As difficult as it may be, they must make an attempt to get involved in their children's lives and therefore participate in their activities as part of their transformation process. Simple gestures, like building a brick house with their young children or taking their teenagers out fishing or playing football, etc., could seriously extinguish the evil fire in the abuser's mind. Children feel loved and cared for when a parent or primary caregiver shows an interest in them.

Apart from helping men bond with their children, this could serve as a buffer or a distraction when the abuser gets emotionally worked up. Aside from that, it makes the child feel comfortable hanging around their father. They learn to do this effortlessly, and they make it a part of their life. They grow up with the experience of a memorable childhood with their father getting involved in their life. Most abusers do not even know what their children's favourite meals are, not to mention their interests, aspirations and dreams. They have no concept of fatherhood because they are consumed by their egoism. But they then expect recognition for their children's achievements later in life.

Recognition comes with responsibilities. This is never convenient for anyone, and it differentiates fathers from sperm donors. Many sperm donors around the world claim to know their rights over their children, but they have no clue of what their responsibilities are or what it takes to raise a child and they do not live up to their obligations as a parent. One of the best ways that men can train their children is to become a role model by being responsible, warm, loving and kind, not only to their children but to other people in their sphere.

Once an abuser is in the process of reformation and has learned to accept their faults, mistakes and becomes sympathetic and rational, their children will automatically learn these positive attributes and apply them in their own lives. It is never too late to begin, and no matter how deep the problem is, taking small steps to correct mistakes of the past goes a long way. This is where healing comes in, not just for those who have been abused but for the abuser himself. When talking about "fathers", I also refer to stepfathers who play a fatherly role in their stepchildren's lives. Until they see themselves as a father, they will never develop a bond or any positive relationship with those children.

As mentioned earlier on, fathers play a vital role in children's lives, but this does not mean that couples should remain together if their relationship is damaged and irreparable. Responsible fathers can still make a positive contribution to their children's lives, even if they do not live together. Research in the US, UK, Asia, and Africa shows that male children are more inclined to pick up their father's traits. They see their father as a "hero" that they would like to emulate. Needless to say, if children are consistently exposed to violence and abuse or are abused by the same father figure, this instils a different mindset in these children, who later in life exhibit the same abusive traits as their fathers.

When men handle problems and misunderstandings in a very mature and civilised manner, it helps shape their children's behaviour towards others, especially their partners in adulthood. Sensible men consistently make a positive effort to shape and form positive characteristics in their children. This is why it's crucial to set an example by doing away with abuse and learning to resolve matters in a more mature and civilised way—with love rather than resorting to abusive and violent behaviour.

•   Incorporating valuable principles

The Center for Parenting Education: Using Your Values to Raise Caring, Responsible, Resilient Children have given this definition: "Value is the amount of worth ascribed to something, the degree to which something is prized or has merit. Values are the beliefs that each person considers are important for himself and possibly for humanity as a whole". When parents incorporate values and abide by them, they indirectly teach their children to do the same; likewise, the children learn and abide by the same values.

Understanding the concept of values and the importance of teaching children about them gives parents a powerful way to influence the child and to shield them from the adverse forces they may encounter in the outside world. This is why abusers have to get to know their children and their goals; this will help them to decide how to relate to their children. Knowledge and values direct the choices parents make in guiding and shaping the behaviours and attitudes they want to reinforce in their children. Without having a clear list of priorities and without working honestly and openly with their partner and children, men struggle to shape their children's behaviours and characters.

Values change with time, gender, age, children's needs and experiences. Some values become less important as others become more important, depending on the children's development and their parents' expectations. Parents may value different attributes at different times in their children, i.e., they may prefer infants as they are not as mobile and may not appreciate the energy children have when they are toddlers, actively exploring their environment. Knowing the different developmental stages of children is key and it takes time to fully understand them. As children go through these stages, they learn from their primary caregivers and mimic their behaviour.

It is around the early stages of children's lives that values can be instilled so they grow up to become responsible, respectful and sensible individuals who can differentiate between right or wrong. While parents may want their children to live according to their values, teenagers can be challenging in the sense that they push boundaries in order to determine their own value system. This is where reformed abusers have to put into practice what they learned from their rehabilitation or therapeutic services by handling their teen children with patience, love and guidance instead of abuse or arrogance.

Intentionality is needed during this process as most of the interactions cannot be planned for or crammed into a few minutes of "quality time". Most opportunities to teach or model moral values arise naturally. This is why it is important for parents to spend quality time with their children, so they do not miss out on teachable moments when they occur. This will not happen if the children's father is not acquainted with these basic but crucial principles that are vital for their upbringing.

Final Word

Amela Puljek-Shank, writing on the topic of trauma and reconciliation, used a powerful metaphor of "the volcano, destruction and rebirth". She stated that, in her view, trauma is similar to a volcanic eruption. "Before the eruption, the volcano is working within—the fire is active, lava is hot, and it is constantly boiling. There is always a certain kind of volcanic activity present (and this is an active volcano we are talking about) that builds up pressure within. After some time, this pressure fills all the space within the volcano and is bursting with the need to 'spend' the pressure.

After a while, this constant level of energy, that cannot be 'spent', collects within the volcano, within a closed space, and it starts to build up to the point that it brings an eruption. The eruption of the volcano is extremely dangerous and destructive—it burns everything on the ground and life is gone. Everything is grey, dark and burnt. The place where lava is present is hot and a lot of poisonous gases are emitted into the air. The place becomes poisonous and death and destruction prevails".

Indeed, when going through traumatic experiences in life, particularly domestic abuse/violence in this case, everything looks gloomy and hopeless. It seems that no one understands and no one ever will. Whilst no one can fully comprehend the depth of emotional, physical and psychological wounds and scars inflicted on women by abusive men, with appropriate support in place, the partner and their children can learn to enjoy a meaningful life again. Many women who go through abuse try to find a way to live through these experiences, to survive them, and to find new meaning in life. However, these experiences can change the course of their lives forever.

They begin to see life in a different light—whether negative or positive—and their perspective shapes their future and approach.

Like in Amela's volcano example, "destruction was severe—the hurt and suffering brought excruciating pain. We felt that we would never be able to live again and that there is no reason to hope and love. However, somewhere deep inside of us, the seeds of life were not destroyed, and despite our desire, they started pushing us to learn and live again—to hope and love. These seeds helped us to heal and find new meaning in life as well as a new sense of purpose. We rose from the ashes of volcanic activity (from its poisonous gases and destruction) and somehow without our knowing how, hope and love poured the rain of life over us, and we rose from the dead—we started to learn how to live again".

It is common in our society to hear people labelling traumatised and abused women as "abnormal", "crazy", "not able to manage difficulties or not able to get over them". These perceptions create a stigma and prejudice for those who are struggling with trauma. They make women perceive their problems as abnormal and eventually view themselves as having personal weaknesses, thereby causing them to take the blame for what is not their fault.

Amela asserted "traumatic experiences have been present in people's lives throughout the centuries and are nothing new or unheard of. The usual ways of dealing with the traumatic experience were to not talk about it, deny it and repress it or try to forget about it. This way of dealing with the traumatic experience is common across cultures. Traumatic experiences are ones that individuals or groups have survived, and they came as a result of violent conflict, rape, physical violence, sexual violence, refugee life, childhood abuse, natural disasters and other life experiences".

It goes without saying that despite the vast number of programmes and support agencies available to help partners and families address the global domestic abuse/violence crisis, some organisations and social groups still sugar-coat the truth and find it difficult to address this problem. Thousands of women are being killed and murdered by abusers across the world, leaving motherless children to suffer at the hands of abusers who get away with murder and carry on with their perverse actions without guilt or remorse. It is time this massacre is brought to light and dealt with accordingly. Abusers hurt inside, and instead of addressing their deep pain and trauma, they go about abusing innocent souls.

In order for abusers to deal with and heal from their trauma, they need to work through their traumatic experiences, as discussed earlier. Amela further declared "There are two ways of walking through trauma. The first one is remembering and repeating the story of traumatic experience over and over again in which the pain and suffering are locked and do not have a way of getting out of the person or a groups' body, mind and soul. A person and a group are trapped in this cycle that can go on for a long time and sometimes even forever. In this case, the trauma creates negative energy that recycles itself within a person or group in a way that creates an eruption which is violent and destructive. We all know people and groups who have not recovered from the traumatic experience(s) and thus were never able to get out of this vicious cycle. They got stuck in their pain and there was no way out of it".

"A violent eruption ended in conflict or war that in turn fed the violence back which would erupt into violence again—and the cycle goes on where we re-traumatise ourselves and thus the violence continues. A second way of working on traumatic experience calls for healing of trauma in a very holistic way. It calls for healing of our mind, body and soul. This requires serious work and dedication on the part of an individual and a group, and it becomes a personal choice on an individual and group level to heal the trauma instead of repeating the trauma through generations. This personal decision does not drop out of a clear sky. Instead, it comes through a process of 'having enough' of violence and destruction.

It comes through the desire to become human again that can live in harmony with ourselves and with others. Once the choice has been made, it becomes clear that this will be a long process that can last for years; it is not quick, and it does not give fast results".

This shows that no matter how deep both the abuser and his victim think they have gone or no matter how helpless their circumstances may look, there is help out there. They need to reach out to the relevant people or agencies that will guide them through their healing journey. Stop living in denial and break the cycle of abuse by seeking counselling, therapy and by talking to trusted people or family members who may offer support in addressing the problem.

This will lead to the abuser loving and valuing himself, so he will be able to love, respect and value his spouse, children and their wider family. Abusers should strive to become good examples to their children or stepchildren by allowing the behavioural modification process to take its course as they take one step at a time, applying the advice, views and opinions of the people supporting them on this journey. Like Amela said, "A place of death and destruction becomes a place of rebirth and life" where all parties involved live freely and without stress and fear of the male figures in their lives.

About the author

Veronica is a social worker by profession and has worked with children and families for a significant number of years. Having experienced domestic abuse and violence herself in her adulthood, she developed a passion for eradication domestic abuse and violence towards women and children. She is now an advocate for domestic abuse victims and is dedicated to supporting and empowering those who are going through abuse directly or indirectly. This passion extends to those who inflict pain and grief on their spouse because they have deep unresolved wounds. Amongst other things, Veronica's desire is for all mankind to live in peace and joy as they journey through life.

Printed in Great Britain
by Amazon

47154850R00086